The Development of Abstractionism in the Writings of Gertrude Stein

GERTRUDE STEIN
(Painting by Pablo Picasso. The Metropolitan Museum of Art,
Bequest of Gertrude Stein, 1946.)

The Development of Abstractionism in the Writings of Gertrude Stein

MICHAEL J. HOFFMAN

Philadelphia
University of Pennsylvania Press

7518
Printed in the United States of America

For Cynthia and Matthew
—my other children

Acknowledgments

My thanks are due the following for granting me permission to quote from copyrighted or unpublished materials:

The Estate of Gertrude Stein, for *Geography and Plays* (Boston: Four Seas Press, 1922); *A Long Gay Book,* in *Matisse Picasso and Gertrude Stein* (Paris: Plain Edition, 1932); *The Making of Americans* (Paris: Contact Editions, 1925); *Picasso* (London: B. T. Batsford, 1948); *Things as They Are* (Pawlet, Vt.: Banyan Press, 1950). Permissions granted by Donald Gallup, Literary Agent for the Gertrude Stein Estate.

And for permission to quote from the following unpublished manuscripts in the Yale Collection of American Literature: "American Language and Literature;" Letter to Alfred Stieglitz, May 6, 1912; early draft of *The Making of Americans.* Permissions granted by Donald Gallup.

The Exposition Press, for *Gertrude Stein: Form and Intelligibility,* by Rosalind S. Miller, copyright 1949 by Exposition Press. Permission granted by Exposition Press.

Little, Brown and Co., for *The Third Rose,* by John Malcolm Brinnin, copyright, 1959, by John Malcolm Brinnin. Permission granted by Little, Brown, and Co.

Oxford University Press, for *James Joyce,* by Richard Ellmann, copyright 1959 by Richard Ellmann. Permission granted by Oxford University Press.

Random House, Inc., for *Lectures in America,* by Gertrude Stein, copyright 1935 by Random House, Inc.; *Portraits and Prayers,* by Gertrude Stein, copyright 1934 by Modern Library, Inc.; *Selected Writings of Gertrude Stein,* by Gertrude Stein, copyright 1946 by Random House, Inc.; *Three Lives,* by Gertrude Stein, copyright 1936 by Gertrude Stein. Permissions granted by Random House, Inc.

University of Oklahoma Press, for *Art by Subtraction,* by B. L. Reid, copyright 1958 by University of Oklahoma Press. Permission granted by University of Oklahoma Press.

Yale University Press, for *Four in America,* by Gertrude Stein, copyright 1947 by Alice B. Toklas; *Two: Gertrude Stein and Her Brother and Other Writings,* by Gertrude Stein, copyright 1951 by Alice B. Toklas; *Gertrude Stein: A Biography of Her Work,* by Donald Sutherland, copyright 1951 by Yale University Press. Permissions granted by Yale University Press.

American Quarterly, for permission to reprint in substantially the same form an article of mine, "Gertrude Stein in the Psychology Laboratory," that appeared in the issue of Spring, 1965. Permission granted by the editor.

Preface

BECAUSE THE PUBLICATION OF UNRIPENED DOCTORAL DISsertations has become an obscenity in the academic world, many writers have taken to hiding behind such euphemisms as, "This study was first begun . . ." and "In an early stage I received the supervision of . . ." In deference to Gertrude Stein, who tried so hard to make people call things by their rightful names, I cannot justify disguising the origins of this book. So, for better or worse, I hereby admit that it was originally a thesis submitted to the English Department of the University of Pennsylvania as part of its requirements for the Ph.D. It has of course been rewritten and is, I hope, sufficiently ripe.

I have been interested in Gertrude Stein for quite a while. Aside from the fascination of her life, it has always seemed incredible to me that someone so well known could be so little read. I became convinced by my own researches into the Stein "myth" that an understanding of her works had been made almost impossible by the partisanship pro and con of those who came to the altar both to worship and to ridicule and by the publicity-conscious manipulations of Miss Stein herself. A study was needed that consciously set out not to take an evaluative stand, but to concentrate almost totally on what was going on in the writings themselves. Gertrude Stein was too important a figure not to deserve some understanding as an artist apart from the imposing figure she cast over the literary history of the twentieth century.

At this point, it seemed obvious to me that a rigorous ordering of materials was in order. Together with Professor Robert E. Spiller I decided to limit my study to the first ten years of Miss Stein's works. The main reasons for this limitation were the large bulk of her writings and the fact that *Tender Buttons* seemed the logical culmination of a series of steadily more abstract works.

The book as it now stands is largely a product of the above ideas. The notion of critical detachment is largely a pose, but it is, I think, a useful one. My aim is not to justify the works of Gertrude Stein, but to discover what they are all about. To do this, I feel it is necessary to stay away from arguing about whether she was a genuis or a phony. I am not interested in the ranking of authors and I do not propose any of her works as literary "touchstones." But it seems to me that we cannot get very far in understanding this strange literary period, the twentieth century, without coming at least partially to terms with Gertrude Stein's writings. If I have succeeded in making these works a bit more comprehensible, the reader will judge for himself.

At this point it is customary to acknowledge the aid of friends, colleagues, and wife. This is a convention I feel no qualms about following because I have received much valuable help and advice. Thanks and acknowledgement must be given to the following: Donald C. Gallup, Gertrude Stein's literary executor and director of the Yale

Collection of American Literature, whose cooperation enabled my short stay at Yale to be quite profitable; the Yale University Library for permission to quote from an unpublished letter of Gertrude Stein to Alfred Stieglitz; Ira Einhorn for his ideas and encouragement; Professor Morse Peckham for discussing Gertrude Stein with me and for impressing on me the usefulness of a construct to attack the writings; Professors Herbert Howarth and Bruce Olsen for careful readings of the manuscript and for valuable suggestions; Mrs. Natsue Kobayashi, able typist; and Professor Nathan Smith who suffered with me through most of the writing, who challenged some of my ideas, and whose sense of humor constantly reminded me that other things in the world were as important as Gertrude Stein's abstractionism.

Thanks especially go to Professor Robert E. Spiller, who originally inspired me to do the book and helped me to organize the materials; whose advice was almost always to the point; and whose enthusiasm has been my major source of gratification. And to Dianna Hoffman, who watched this book grow as I grew, who typed two of its drafts, endured my fits of temperament and depression, and still managed to get dinner on the table in time.

May, 1965
Philadelphia, Pa.

Contents

The Development of Abstractionism in the Writings of Gertrude Stein

1

Introduction

THIS BOOK IS NEITHER AN APOLOGY FOR NOR A DAMNA-
tion of Gertrude Stein. If it seems foolish to begin with
such a profession, I can only say that almost every attempt
to deal with the work of Gertrude Stein has fallen into one
or the other of these traps. I am less concerned with taking sides than with examining a phenomenon. The one
area of common agreement about Gertrude Stein's writings is that they are "abstract." It is the phenomenon of
her abstractionism that I propose to examine, specifically
the progressive development of this abstractionism in her
early writings.

Gertrude Stein was not born an abstractionist. She
reached her so-called "mature style" only through long
and conscious effort. Her earliest writings fall into that
general mode of prose narrative usually termed realism.
Things as They Are, the posthumously published first
novel, and *Three Lives* can still claim a family relation-

ship with the later Henry James and the early Joyce. But
The Making of Americans, the early "portraits," and
Tender Buttons explore areas in which no other writer in
the English language had yet set foot. In what ways do
Gertrude Stein's earliest writings show abstractionist tendencies? What stylistic shifts lead her writings down the
path of abstractionism to non-representationalism?

Gertrude Stein's abstractionism was a part of the cultural milieu of the time. The first decade of the twentieth
century saw profound revolutions in all the arts and sci-
ences. In 1905 Einstein first published his Theory of Rela-
tivity. At the same time Bergson was giving his lectures on
Creative Evolution; Russell and Whitehead were writing
Principia Mathematica; and William James had for the
past decade and more been expounding his doctrine of
Radical Empiricism and his theories of the stream of consciousness. It was also at this time that the Fauves began
to exhibit their tradition-shattering paintings, only to be
followed a few years later by the cubism of Braque and
Picasso. And in music Schönberg began to develop his se-
rial technique in his early quartets and his *Five Pieces for
Orchestra.* It was a decade in which all the arts and scien-
ces developed new ways of looking at the world. These
are factors that we must keep in mind throughout our consideration of the stylistic development of Miss Stein's
early writings. We shall be discussing the influence of
painting on Miss Stein's writings in the later chapters,
and in an appendix we shall explore two of the most
important intellectual sources for her peculiar notions of
personality, time, flux, and repetition.

The scope of the study will be limited to the years,
1903-1913. There are two good reasons for this limita-

tion. The first and obvious reason is a spatial one. Gertrude Stein's collected *opera* are so voluminous that one could not hope to cover them all adequately in the space of a book of modest length. The second and more important reason is that the decade chosen forms somewhat of an organic unit in covering all the major stylistic changes that led Gertrude Stein to abstractionism. The only major change in the style of Gertrude Stein's creative writings after this decade was in the development of her idiosyncratic notions of drama, as in the well-known *Four Saints in Three Acts*. However, there are few concepts in her plays that she had not at least explored in her first decade of writing; and this first decade contains not only her most stylistically significant works, but her best-known ones as well (except for *The Autobiography of Alice B. Toklas*, which, as a memoir, is of a totally different kind of subject matter as well as style).

It should be made clear that I am concerned with dates of composition rather than publication. Because of the difficulties that Gertrude Stein encountered early in her career trying to find her way into print, most of her writing was not published until years after composition. *Things as They Are* was written in 1903 but not published until 1950, four years after Gertrude Stein's death. *Three Lives* was composed in 1905-06 and published in 1909. *The Making of Americans* was written between 1906 and 1911, but did not see print until 1925. The only ones of Gertrude Stein's early writings published almost immediately after creation were *The Portrait of Mabel Dodge at the Villa Curonia*, written and published in 1912, and *Tender Buttons*, finished in 1913 and published the following year. Some of the pieces, such as *Two: Gertrude Stein and Her Brother,* did not see print until the Yale University Press began to issue Gertrude Stein's unpublished manuscripts in 1951.

The position that Gertrude Stein occupies in the literary hierarchy is perhaps unique among the so-called "important" figures in modern literature, in that she has been the subject of almost no adequate literary criticism. Although she is often linked off-handedly with James Joyce as one of the two great stylistic innovators of English in this century, nothing comparable to the "Joyce industry"[1] has sprung up about her work. It may be, as one critic has said recently, that there is ten times as much Joyce criticism because Joyce is ten times the better writer.[2] However, there is another reason that seems more likely. Gertrude Stein's writings do not fit into the mainstream of twentieth-century criticism. The modern man of letters is largely a product of the influences of analytic psychology, both Freudian and Jungian, and cultural anthropology, especially of Fraser and his followers. He is inclined to look at literature primarily in terms of its symbolism, both analytic and archetypal, and its use of myth and ritual. The students of Joyce have a seemingly inexhaustible well from which to nourish their own particular orientation toward literature, especially in *Ulysses* and *Finnegans Wake.* But the student of Gertrude Stein is offered slim rewards in this direction, for in her conscious drive toward abstraction Miss Stein reduced the psychologic and mythic overtones of her writing to such an extent that their occasional appearance seems almost accidental. If in Joyce's writing subject matter is so enriched that almost

[1] Vivian Mercier, "In Joyce's Wake, A Booming Industry," *New York Times Book Rev.,* LXVI (July 30, 1961), 5, 20-1.

[2] Ben Reid, *Art by Subtraction: A Dissenting Opinion of Gertrude Stein* (Norman, Okla., 1958), p. 3.

any allusion may have innumerable possible referents, then in Gertrude Stein the subject is ultimately reduced almost to non-existence and seemingly nothing is left but pure sound and syntax. It is ostensibly a task for the philologist, and the student of literature has continually thrown up his hands in despair at writing that he simply does not "understand."

Whatever the reason for the critical famine surrounding Gertrude Stein, the truth is that there have been only two full-length books of genuine worth on the subject. The first is Donald Sutherland's *Biography of Her Work*,[3] a critical accompaniment to the Yale series of Miss Stein's unpublished manuscripts. This is an exasperating, though constantly stimulating, *apologia* for Gertrude Stein and for modern art in general. It suffers seriously from its polemical attitude and Mr. Sutherland's obvious feeling that he is called upon to defend everything and anything Stein. His passionate involvement with his subject does not lead to consistently lucid exposition of the difficulties of the writing, but as a justification of the modern movements in writing and painting the book is one of the important documents of modern criticism. The challenge it presents will certainly have to be met by any future critical studies of Gertrude Stein.

The other book of value is John Malcolm Brinnin's biography, *The Third Rose: Gertrude Stein and Her World*.[4] Aside from being a valuable "life," it contains hundreds of provocative comments on Gertrude Stein's writing, twentieth-century painting, and modern intellectual and artistic movements in general; and it does not suffer from the over-enthusiastic cultism that infects Mr.

[3] *Gertrude Stein: A Biography of Her Work* (New Haven, 1951).
[4] Boston, 1959.

Sutherland. It should certainly be a source book of Gertrude Stein scholarship for years to come.

After these two books there is very little of value, except for some shorter pieces. Thornton Wilder's introduction to *Four in America*[5] is critically useful with regard to Gertrude Stein's aesthetic theories. An article by Allegra Stewart[6] is important for its insights into Miss Stein's intellectual relationships with the three great thinkers who influenced her most: Bergson, Whitehead, and William James. A recent article by Richard Bridgman[7] contains valuable insights into "Melanctha." And Frederick J. Hoffman's monograph, *Gertrude Stein,*[8] provides the best short introduction to the subject, although it is too general for more than that.

In addition to the above, one of the three unpublished doctoral dissertations[9] that have been completed on Gertrude Stein has some critical merit. H. R. Garvin has attempted to trace the relationship between Miss Stein's critical writings and her actual creative output. The opening chapters on the cultural and intellectual background are valuable; the chapters on the writings themselves much less so.

There are four other books on the subject which ought to be mentioned. W. G. Rogers' memoir, *When This You*

[5] "Introduction," *Four in America,* by Gertrude Stein (New Haven, 1947).

[6] "Quality of Gertrude Stein's Creativity," *Am. Lit.,* XXVIII (Jan. 1957), 488-506.

[7] "Melanctha," *Am. Lit.,* XXXIII (Nov. 1961), 350-9.

[8] U. of Minnesota Pamphlets, No. 10 (Minneapolis, 1961).

[9] H. R. Garvin, "Gertrude Stein: A Study of Her Theory and Practice" (Michigan, 1950); Wilford Leach, "Gertrude Stein and the Modern Theatre" (Illinois, 1956); Frederick W. Lowe, "Gertrude's Web: A Study of Gertrude Stein's Literary Relationships" (Columbia, 1957).

See Remember Me,[10] has only anecdotal interest concerning his friendship with Miss Stein, and is of no critical
value. *Gertrude Stein: Form and Intelligibility,* by
Rosalind S. Miller,[11] is a general introduction that is almost worthless except for the inclusion of Miss Stein's
Radcliffe themes, which are reprinted at the end. Elizabeth Sprigge's biography[12] is interesting only as a life,
making almost no effort at criticism. As a biography it is
superseded in all respects by Brinnin's.

The fourth book is Ben Reid's *Art by Subtraction: A
Dissenting Opinion of Gertrude Stein,* which attempts to
be the *bête noire* of Gertrude Stein criticism. Mr. Reid
has decided once and for all to banish Miss Stein from
literature, and he spends an entire book attempting to
justify his point of view. Because his thinking is sympto-
matic of so much that has been wrong in so many attempts to deal with Gertrude Stein, it will be worthwhile
to quote a passage in full from his book.

It seems to me that Miss Stein is a vulgar genius talking to
herself, and if she is talking to herself, she is not an artist. It is
because she does talk to herself that she offers insuperable
difficulties to both reader and critic. I suggest, therefore, that
she be defined out of existence as an artist. To be an artist, she
must talk to us, not to the dullest or the most tradition bound
or the most unsympathetic of us, but to those of us who are
flexible, those willing to be fruitfully led. There is not world
enough or time enough for Gertrude Stein's kind of writing;
too much in literature is both excellent and knowable.[13]

It is obvious from the above passage that Gertrude
Stein does not "talk" to Mr. Reid. Like an old woman

---

[10] New York, 1948.
[11] New York, 1949.
[12] *Gertrude Stein: Her Life and Work* (New York, 1957).
[13] Reid, *op. cit.,* pp. 170-1. From *Art by Subtraction* by B. L. Reid.
Copyright 1958 by the University of Oklahoma Press.

who cannot tolerate foreigners because they talk in a strange tongue, Mr. Reid proposes to excommunicate Gertrude Stein to another realm than "art." This is the rhetoric of a frustrated man, who has elevated his inability to cope with the writings before him into a universal condemnation of them as art. There would be little point in quoting the above passage were it not so typical of reactions to the writing of Gertrude Stein. But the standard reaction, after an initial amused condescension, is like Mr. Reid's. In the next stage the reader resorts to accusations such as "phony" and "charlatan." Mr. Reid is obviously familiar with the fable about the emperor's clothing and he eschews this kind of excoriation, although one always has the feeling that he would like to resort to some good old-fashioned name-calling. In addition, although Mr. Reid proposes to discuss Gertrude Stein as a creative artist, he spends 75 per cent or more of his time with her critical or "straightforward" works. Most attempts to criticize the writings of Gertrude Stein share this characteristic. Critics have, for the most part, not been able to find a language with which to discuss her fictional prose and poetry, and so they resort to taking issue with her pithy and often exasperating critical statements rather than make an honest confrontation of her more difficult writings.

The task of the student of Gertrude Stein is always complicated by the fact of her overwhelming personality. The "myth" of Gertrude Stein has always overshadowed her writings. "It always did bother me that the American public were more interested in me than in my work,"[14] she

[14] Gertrude Stein, *Everybody's Autobiography* (New York, 1937), p. 50.

lamented late in her career, but she more than anyone else made herself into a "personality." She was the head of a salon in Paris, hobnobber with the fashionable painters and writers, leader of a literary cult, self-styled pontiff of modern letters, and symbol of the expatriation of the post World War I American artist. She was the object of either unbounded admiration or passionate resentment, almost exclusively through reaction to her as a person rather than to her writings. As a result, her critical reputation has been the victim of partisanship.

As we have seen, most of the writings on Gertrude Stein try to do one of two things: either prove that she is the greatest author of the century (Sutherland, Julian Sawyer,[15] Rogers) or show her up as a charlatan (Reid, Richard Aldington,[16] Hilary Corke[17]). Everyone who writes as much as a line on the subject feels called upon to take sides. As a result, critics have spent most of their time judging and almost none of their time trying to develop a critical method equipped to handle the problems posed by Miss Stein's writing. What is going on in Gertrude Stein's work? This is the question that no one has yet seriously examined and that this writer now proposes to investigate. What are the central qualities indigenous to her writing, and how do they develop chronologically through her early works? It seems to me that once we have established the nature of her achievement we will then be in a position for the first time to make normative judgments as to her value as an artist.

[15] *Gertrude Stein: A Bibliography* (New York, 1941).
[16] "The Disciples of Gertrude Stein," *Poetry,* XVII (Oct. 1920), 35-40.
[17] "Reflections on a Great Stone Face: The Achievement of Gertrude Stein," *Kenyon Rev.,* XXIII (Summer 1961), 367-389.

For the methodological purposes of this examination I accept wholeheartedly the distinctions that Northrop Frye makes in *Anatomy of Criticism* concerning the critical and evaluative modes of criticism. By critical method Mr. Frye refers primarily to descriptive examination of texts. Evaluative method is predominantly concerned with value judgments. Although Mr. Frye is well aware that the two modes cannot in any pure sense be separated, he nonetheless calls for an awareness of the distinction between the two and for statements on the part of critics as to what their critical aims are in relation to the above modes.[18] In the light of the above description, I then propose to do a critical study of the first decade of Gertrude Stein's writing, since the evaluative critics have obviously been unequal to the job. This is not to say that I have no opinions on the subject; to the contrary. But I feel that more is to be gained by suppressing value judgments and adopting a cool, analytic attitude. I much prefer adopting an evaluative attitude toward the evaluative critics who have not bothered to examine carefully either their assumptions or the writings of Gertrude Stein.

Keeping the above strictures carefully in mind, I shall now make my one totally evaluative statement of this entire study, doing so only to justify going on with the project at all. I make the assumption for the purposes of this study that Gertrude Stein is a serious, important, and influential writer whose work has not received the correspondingly serious attention that it deserves. I make no assumptions as to whether she is either a "good" or an "interesting" writer. Perhaps an understanding of

[18] For a full discussion of the above points see Mr. Frye's "Polemical Introduction," *Anatomy of Criticism* (Princeton, 1957).

the abstract nature of her writing will provide an implicit answer, one way or the other, to such value judgments.

The analysis of Gertrude Stein's style will be predominantly concerned with formal and linguistic elements. It will not be an attempt to reduce the more difficult writings, such as *Tender Buttons,* to a kind of Basic English, but it will rather attempt to show, for one, how she violates basic syntax and to what purpose she does so. Another related problem it will attempt to explore, for example, will be her use of repetition, both in sentence structure and subject matter, as a mirroring of the psychic state of her characters (in *Three Lives*), as a reflection of the "continuous present" (*The Making of Americans*), and as a linguistic abstraction that reflects the abstraction in plot and character development. However, the approach will not be an exclusively "new critical" one. To understand Gertrude Stein purely in terms of verbal elements is to have only a partial inkling of her significance to twentieth-century writing. She is, even more than most, the product of her time. To make this cliché stand up, this book will endeavor to show that almost all the intellectual and artistic movements of the time find some reflection in the writing of Gertrude Stein. Even her personality reflects the militant emancipation of women characteristic of the "feminist" generation. At the psychology laboratories of Harvard and Radcliffe she learned from Hugo Münsterberg and William James the then-emerging concepts of the human consciousness and unconscious, continuing her explorations of these areas in original work of her own on auto-

matic writing.[19] The effects of these influences are to be
seen largely in her concept of personality, particularly as
manifested in *Three Lives* and *The Making of Americans.* The scientific attitude which she exhibits in so
much of her writing certainly had a substantial part of
its origin at Harvard and in the four years she spent at
the Johns Hopkins medical school, where she did re-
search on the physiology of the brain.

The affinities with modern painting that so many critics have pointed out in her writings have a substantial
grounding in fact. Gertrude Stein and her brothers Leo
and Mike can claim, at least as much as anyone else, the
"discovery" of Matisse and Picasso in the first five years
of the new century. These "discoveries" turned into
friendships with the artists, and an introduction into the
artistic community of contemporary Paris. The relationship with Picasso turned into a close and intimate one
(though platonic), in which two congenial minds influenced one another. The growing influence of modern
painting can be seen in the early portraits and especially
in *Tender Buttons,* in which Gertrude Stein attempted
her own verbal collage. It can also be seen in the approach Miss Stein took to her art. Like the major painters, Picasso and Matisse, she set up a specific problem in
each one of her performances. On the successful solution
of the problem, she, like the painters, moved on to new

[19] See two articles that Gertrude Stein published summarizing re-
search that she had done at Harvard under the supervision of William
James: Gertrude Stein and Leon M. Solomons, "Normal Motor
Automatism," *Psychological Rev.,* III (Sept. 1896), 492-512, and
Gertrude Stein, "Cultivated Motor Automatism," *Psychological Rev.,*
V (May 1898), 295-306. These are Miss Stein's first published writ-
ings.

areas of exploration and new problems. One sees this even in a contemporary composer such as Stravinsky. Once again in affinity with the painters, she considered herself freed from the previous tradition of her art. She thought of herself as breaking off completely from the previous practitioners of the *belles lettres* and creating, as it were, a new tradition with each new piece of writing, in much the same way as her good friend Picasso did in painting.

And Gertrude Stein shared with her contemporaries Joyce and Proust the concern with time that Wyndham Lewis and others[20] have found so characteristic of the writers of the modern age. Eschewing Joyce's concern with myth and historical cycles and Proust's obsession with memory, Miss Stein is primarily concerned with the concept of the continuous and ongoing present to which she was first exposed at Harvard under William James, later at Bergson's lectures at the Collège de France, and still later as a personal friend of Alfred North White-head. The influences expecially of the first two are important to her early writings. This problem and the previous two will be discussed at greater length in the body of the study. I have gone through these sketchy outlines mainly to show that Gertrude Stein's experiments are not an isolated phenomenon and that the grounds of any study of her as an artist must have a broader base than just the writings themselves.

One problem still remains before we can examine the specific questions at hand. The term "abstraction" (and

---

[20] Wyndham Lewis, *Time and Western Man* (New York, 1928); Hans Meyerhoff, *Time in Literature* (Berkeley and Los Angeles, 1955).

its various forms) that we have been using rather freely in this opening chapter must be defined in the terms that we are going to be using it in the remaining body of the text. Actually, what I am going to propose is more in the nature of a construct than a dictionary definition. I am less concerned with its lexical "truth" than I am with its usefulness as an instrument in attacking the problems posed by Gertrude Stein.

Among the definitions of the noun "abstraction" on page eight of Webster's *Third International Unabridged Dictionary* appears the following: "the act or process of leaving out of consideration one or more qualities of a complex object so as to attend to others." Under this definition we can subsume, for all practical purposes, the characteristics of abstractionism that appear in the early writings of Gertrude Stein. Her writings, almost from the very beginning, are characterized in style and subject matter by a progressive "leaving-out" of elements normally appearing in the works of most of her American contemporaries and immediate European predecessors. In terms of the "complex object" of realistic verisimilitude, for instance, Gertrude Stein from the beginning left out the small detail and careful description of externals that the realists had long used to convey the illusion of reality. During the same decade in which Theodore Dreiser was finally displaying the triumph of naturalism in the American novel (a victory that European novelists had won over three decades earlier), his fellow American Gertrude Stein was writing, in Paris, the absolute antithesis of the naturalistic novel in her static character studies in which people are described in long circular sentences or in which they merely talk interminably about themselves and their problems. The first effect of this "art by subtraction,"[21] then, is the loss of the traditional verisimilitude of the realistic novel.

Carrying this further, one can see the effect of the loss of verisimilitude on the style of the writing. The easy flow of the transparent author is sacrificed to a style that constantly refers back to itself and forward to events not to be known until much later,[22] or juxtaposes apparently unrelated elements. The destruction of realistic verisimilitude and the easy flowing style are progressive elements in Gertrude Stein's abstractionism and can be traced in a chronological fashion throughout her early work.

There is also a steady subtraction of all elements that convey the idea of physical movement. In terms of the traditional plot, nothing "happens" in Gertrude Stein. People talk, they are described, we see them change subtly. But the closer she moved toward her descriptions of the "essences" of people and things, as in the portraits and *Tender Buttons,* the less she felt she had to make people and things "do"; they merely had to "be."

Another element of Gertrude Stein's abstractionism is the abandonment of some of the conventional patterns of verbal communication. Words are often wrenched from

[21] Kenneth Burke was the first to coin this expression (later perverted by Mr. Reid) in connection with the writings of Gertrude Stein in his insightful review of *Geography and Plays,* "Engineering with Words," *Dial,* LXXIV (April 1923), 410. Mr. Burke's usage has a mildly pejorative connotation. I am retaining the phrase as a descriptive term without its previous pejorative baggage.

[22] This "self-reflexive" style characteristic of so much twentieth-century poetry and fiction has received its most perceptive treatment from Joseph Frank in a long essay on "Spatial Form in Modern Literature," *Sewanee Review,* LIII (Summer and Autumn 1945), 221-40, 433-56, 643-53.

ordinary lexical meanings. The statements contained in consecutive sentences may have no ostensible relation to one another, to anything said in the previous paragraph, or to the supposed subject of the writing. She is also perfectly willing to make statements to which only she has the key. In writing portraits of her friends she includes personal facts, idiosyncracies, or statements (without quotation marks) that the subject of the portrait has made which no outside reader will ever be able to understand more than partially.

Other elements of abstractionism include Gertrude Stein's idiosyncratic punctuation, that finally consists of the almost total abandonment of the comma and, very often, the dropping of the capital letter before proper nouns, among other things.

It is to these elements and others similar to them that I refer when I use the term abstractionism in reference to Gertrude Stein's "art by subtraction." Not all the above characteristics will be in play at once in any given piece by Gertrude Stein. The varieties of abstractionism are many in her writing, and they are constantly changing from work to work. It is to the specifically abstract qualities of the individual works and the progressive march toward greater abstraction throughout all the early works that we will be devoting our attention throughout the following pages.

idiosyncratic punctuation is almost non-existent. In contrast to her later "art by subtraction," there appear passages of fully sensual, almost Pateresque description. The book is a good antidote to the comments of those who say that Gertrude Stein could not write standard English, and should serve the same function in this regard as does Joyce's *Dubliners,* Picasso's "Blue Period," and Schönberg's *Verklärte Nacht.* But like these other works to which it bears this particular similarity, *Things as They Are* contains the seeds of the later abstractionism that was to become the hallmark of its creator.

The term abstractionism implies a contrast. For one book to be called abstract, there must be another that is less so to which it may be compared. The term "concrete," which is the usual antithesis to abstract, would obviously be clumsy in this context. In the previous chapter I had chosen as the antithetical quality to abstract, in this particular context, the term "realistic verisimilitude." The pursuit of this quality had been the primary concern of the realists and naturalists who just preceded and were contemporary with Gertrude Stein. To recapture "things as they are" was their aim, an aim which Gertrude Stein also professed to accept, but which she pursued with vastly differing methods and results. (Viewed in this light, the choice of *Things as They Are* as a title by her posthumous editors is ironic indeed.)

Anyone doubting the inherent abstractionism of *Things as They Are* need only compare it to a novel of the antithetic naturalist tradition, such as *Sister Carrie,* to realize the vast difference in aims and methods. Dreiser first published *Sister Carrie* in 1900, but since he had so much difficulty in having the novel released for sale for the next decade, it is virtually certain that Gertrude Stein had not read it when she wrote her first novel. Thus, we can say that she was neither influenced by Dreiser, nor did she write in reaction to what he was doing. They were two authors writing out of the same time, though not necessarily out of exactly the same cultural ambience. Although they are both determinists to more or less a degree, they share virtually nothing in regard to their ways of presenting their narrative. Dreiser's carefully detailed documentation of setting, characterization, conversation, and action find no reflection at all in *Things as They Are,* in which detail is foregone in favor of broadly generalized and shorthand descriptions of the characters and their situation. If Dreiser's type of naturalism is dominant in this period of English and American letters, then Miss Stein's novel diverges very definitely from the dominant tradition, a dominance that was to be challenged increasingly by writers such as James Joyce, Dorothy Richardson, Virginia Woolf, and other progenitors of the stream of consciousness and the novel of personal sensibility.

The main precursor of the novel of sensibility in English and American letters was, of course, Henry James, who had carried the novel of traditional form to the farthest levels of abstractionism it could bear without using stream of consciousness or fragmenting the form as his followers were to do. To James, what happened to his characters was less important than how they reacted to what happened, to themselves, and to one another. The sensibility of the individual in contact with other characters and the shifting nature of social and inter-personal relations among individuals is the subject of the later

James novel. The rendering of action, movement, and small detail is secondary or absent altogether. Viewed in this light, *Things as They Are* is a Jamesian novel, moving against the tradition of *Sister Carrie* but within the tradition of *The Wings of the Dove*. It is concerned not so much with what the characters do, as with how they interact. It is concerned not with realistically portrayed external settings, but with portraying the workings of the minds and sensibilities of its characters. Gertrude Stein denied that she had read Henry James in her early years,[4] but she had obviously forgotten the evidence contained in her "lost" first novel. Mentioning Kate Croy by name, Adele makes a moral comparison between herself and the third member of the triangle of *The Wings of the Dove*.[5] Gertrude Stein obviously knew Henry James' work well at the time she was writing *Things as They Are*. The many similarities between *The Wings of the Dove* and *Things as They Are* may perhaps be accidental, but that Gertrude Stein is following in the tradton of Henry James there can be no doubt.

Things as They Are is basically a conventional novel, setting forth a carefully balanced, though not elaborate, plot with a style that on the surface seems to belong to the writing of its time. To say that it contains the seeds

[4] Gertrude Stein has Alice B. Toklas say in *The Autobiography of Alice B. Toklas* (New York, 1933), p. 78:

> . . . Gertrude Stein contends that Henry James was the first person in literature to find the way to the literary methods of the twentieth century. But oddly enough in all of her formative period she did not read him and was not interested in him.

[5] *Things as They Are*, p. 75. Page numbers subsequently appearing in the text will refer to this edition. If no page number follows quotation, the page is the same as the last number listed in the text. This custom will be followed throughout the book.

of the later abstractionism of Gertrude Stein is not to say that it is basically an abstract novel. It is important to point out its abstract elements only to show the continuity between this earliest work of Gertrude Stein and those that follow it. Had *Things as They Are* not been succeeded by *Three Lives* and *The Making of Americans*, an analysis of its supposed abstractionism would be tenuous at best.

Things as They Are is the story of three young American women—Adele (whose last name we do not know, but whose given name is the sub-title for Book One), Helen Thomas, and Sophie Neathe—who are sailing to Europe at the opening of the book. They are well-to-do, highly educated, and Emancipated. Our introduction to Adele on the first page of the narrative gives us a picture of world-weariness and mild snobbishness. "The last month of Adele's life," the book begins, "had been such a succession of wearing experiences that she rather regretted that she was not to have the steamer all to herself." (3) And a few lines later Adele thinks to herself, "Heigho it's an awful grind; new countries, new people and new experiences all to see, to know and to understand." An effete and supercilious boredom sets the scene for the ensuing triangle.

Before going directly into the narrative proper the third person narrator gives a short individual description of the three women, stating that each of them, though "distinctively American . . . bore definitely the stamp of one of the older civilisations." Helen Thomas is "the American version of the English handsome girl" and Sophie Neathe possesses the "long angular body" which "betrayed her New England origin." These capsule analyses prefigure Gertrude Stein's later overriding concern with types (both racial and personality) that appears most strongly in *The Making of Americans*. Miss Stein states a description of each of the characters. The arch-realist would have displayed these characteristics through the actions and speech of his people. Miss Stein is also quite willing to break the narrative off for commentary or description of her own. On the very first page of the book, she breaks in with an unsolicited comment: "A little knowledge is not a dangerous thing, on the contrary it gives the most cheerful sense of completeness and content." This breaking of the smooth narrative line is an instance of abstractionism that leads ultimately (in *The Making of Americans*) to the almost complete taking over of the narrative by the narrator (i.e., Miss Stein). Gertrude Stein does not care to pretend that no one wrote her books, and she assumes different narrative guises in her various works.

In *Things as They Are* the narrator is on fairly familiar terms with his audience, standing with no attempt to be transparent between the reader and the events and characters he describes. Although the tone is not uniformly consistent, the narrator always gives the impression of having certain information that he is more than willing to impart, along with judgments and general statements that show his superiority to the characters he is describing. There is no attempt here to involve the reader in the creative process, as in *The Making of Americans,* or to disappear into the "narrative tone" of the story, as in "Melanctha." The narrator assumes a place apart from the very fabric of the story, but not far enough apart as to appear totally uninvolved.

After the descriptive passages we first see the characters in a deck-side conversation. Adele, the talkative one, is defending "middle-class ideals" against the protests of the other two. Miss Stein has set the scene with a shorthand minimum of physical description, leaving out such things as the presence of other people on the deck, noises, the motion of the ship, and other physical details that more realistically oriented authors would have included.

Sophie tires of the conversation and gets up to leave. Helen makes an overly polite offer to accompany her back to her steamer chair, whereupon Adele gives the first hint of the Lesbian subject as she says impatiently, "I always did thank God I wasn't born a woman." (7) It is obvious at this point that Sophie and Helen have already established a close relationship, but that there is a growing attraction between Adele and Helen. With Sophie gone, Helen and Adele are left alone on the deck, and we feel for the first time the bond that is heightening between them. After a few moments of talk Helen accuses Adele of being cold, of lacking passion, to which Adele proposes to become Helen's pupil in such matters. The triangle has been set up with almost geometrical precision, with Helen as the pivotal figure in the power struggle between the "slow-moving" Adele and the cool and efficient Sophie.

The attachment between the two grows, with Sophie as a kind of spectator, but Adele's moral reservations prevent her deep emotional involvement. The day before they are to leave the ship Adele suddenly realizes the depth of her feelings for Helen, and the relationship thickens. Adele's moral resistance has broken down, and

Helen reciprocates the affection. In the privacy of the darkened deck she kisses her.

The rest of the book is a working out of the three-way relationship, on which almost all of the narrative focuses. The only reality in the world of *Things as They Are* is that which is contained within the relationships among the three women. In terms of life external to them, the three women seem to live *in vaccuo*. There is no description of physical detail to speak of, either of external reality or of the girls themselves. The three are not only almost completely abstracted from the life around them, but their peculiar interrelationships are abstracted from everything else that is of any consequence in their own personal lives. For the richness of the detailed social portrait is substituted the richness of the pure experience. The technique is that of the closely-knit short story rather than the novel.

The close analysis of individual experience and motives now begins with Adele's mental ruminations over her moral reluctance to commit herself to the type of relationship she seems about to enter into, her concern about Helen's returning the affection it is so difficult for Adele to give, and her second thoughts about the strength of Sophie's control over Helen. Gertrude Stein's almost scientific interest in personality leads her into the most minute explorations of the motives, doubts, forebodings, and second thoughts with which a "slow-moving" person such as Adele must torture herself before making any serious emotional commitment. These mental tossings and turnings are more important to the book than any decision Adele might make in regard to Helen, because what is important to Gertrude Stein is the consciousness of Adele, what makes her tick, what goes through her mind. Adele is inflicting the same self-torture that is standard in any normally heterosexual literary love situation. The flux of the love relationships among the three women is handled in much the same way that Henry James handles the complex emotional relationships of *The Wings of the Dove* and *The Ambassadors,* and it prefigures the vagaries of the relationship between Jeff Campbell and Melanctha in *Three Lives.*

After the three girls split to go through Europe—Helen and Sophie together—Adele's travels are constantly disturbed by the dialogue she continually conducts with herself about her relationship with Helen. Occasional passages of genuinely sensual physical description obtrude as a kind of counterbalance to Adele's inwardness.

Sitting in the court of the Alhambra watching the swallows fly in and out of the crevices of the walls, bathing in the soft air filled with the fragrance of myrtle and oleander and letting the hot sun burn her face and the palms of her hands, losing herself thus in sensuous delight she would murmur again and again 'No it isn't just this, it's something more, something different. I haven't really felt it but I have caught a glimpse.' (17)

Passages such as these are rare, and one often wonders whether they are as much intentional counterbalancing as merely the effusive productions of a still young writer very much in love with words. At this point, Book One comes to an end.

The sub-title of Book Two is "Sophie Neathe," and it opens in Sophie's room in Baltimore. About Sophie's background we are told nothing, but this is also true of

Adele. They obviously have the money to travel and to support homes or rooms of their own, but we must simply take these things for granted, as in the Henry James world. The problem of where money comes from is almost too coarse a matter to be permitted in the pages of a book. The background of only one of the characters, Helen Thomas, is discussed at all. In a conversation between Adele and Sophie we discover that Helen's relationship with her parents is unhappy, and her financial independence of them is not complete. Once, as a girl, Helen had broken her arm, and her father refused to have it treated for a few days. But, just as stubborn as her father, Helen bore the pain stoically, refusing to admit that she was in any discomfort until her father summoned a doctor. And so, Helen is not only anxious to be away from her family, but she is also dependent financially, it is implied, on Sophie Neathe. In discussing Helen, Sophie displays "an implication of ownership" that annoys Adele.

Adele visits Helen in New York, where "for the first time in Adele's experience something happened in which she had no definite consciousness of beginnings. She found herself at the end of a passionate embrace." (28-9)

Over the winter the three girls get together frequently. Sophie realizes now that there is something between the other two, and she tries never to leave them alone together. In subtle ways, she asserts her authority over Helen, and Adele begins to realize how much Helen is bound to Sophie. One evening, at Adele's insistence, Sophie explains exactly what kind of relationship she and Helen are having. The reader is told that Sophie is explaining things, but he never hears the details of the story, and the only way he has of knowing the significance of what Sophie is saying is by the revulsion that Adele feels as she listens: "The room grew large and portentous and to Sophie's eyes Adele's figure grew almost dreadful in its concentrated repulsion." (37)

With what she has just heard from Sophie, Adele feels her revulsion turn against Helen, and she is unable to write to her. Two days before an expected visit from Helen she receives a bitter letter from her accusing her of being petty and complacent. Adele's first reaction is one of anger, but after a short time she relents and writes Helen a conciliatory but unapologetic letter professing once again her devotion.

After a few days of self torture, Adele finally sees Helen once again at an evening performance of *Carmen,* at which Sophie sits between them. A long evening of avoidance heightens Adele's self-doubts as she waits for Helen's inevitable rejection of her. They go to Sophie's apartment, both of them obviously depressed and on edge. They leave together, and on the steps out of Sophie's sight they melt into an embrace. " 'We will certainly have earned our friendship when it is finally accomplished,' Adele said at last." (41)

The following day Sophie comes to see Adele, from whom Helen had wanted the nature of her relationship with Sophie kept a secret. Sophie now informs Adele that she has told Helen that she divulged their secret. She says that Helen was angry at first, but that she has now forgiven Sophie. However, Sophie has lied. Helen is quite unaware of what Adele knows.

On the eve of Adele's departure for Europe she once

again goes to Helen's room. Assuming that Sophie had indeed told Helen what she has admitted to Adele, Adele mentions to Helen the information that Sophie has given her. It is obvious from Helen's angry response that Sophie has not told Helen at all and that she is playing an underhanded game with Adele for Helen's affections. A long moment of brooding silence is broken once again by an embrace.

That summer in Italy Adele realizes how complex mentally and morally she has become in the past year. "In these long lazy Italian days she did not discuss these matters with herself," (44) but "she poured herself out fully and freely to Helen in their ardent correspondence." She wonders if she should be cautious in her letters, knowing that Helen and Sophie are to be together most of the summer. There then comes on the part of Helen a hiatus in the correspondence, and Adele feels that "Sophie has gotten hold of some of the letters and there has been trouble." (47) Her growing awareness of the complexity of the moral situation is intensified by her realization that Helen's financial position makes her very dependent on Sophie. She writes Helen a letter offering her the opportunity to break the relationship, since she feels that she will " 'inevitably cause [her] so much trouble.' " (48) Helen vehemently refuses the offer, promising that Sophie will no longer be jealous of Adele. Adele accepts Helen's decision, knowing, however, that Sophie's jealousy has in no way disappeared and lamenting that " 'how so proud a woman can permit such control is more than I can understand.' " (49)

On this note Book Two comes to an end. The relationships between Helen and Adele and among the three have not become solidified, and none of the problems are at all near resolution or seem to hold any hope of being resolved. And yet, the emotional situation and the power struggle have become extremely complex almost without seeming to do so. The internal growth of Adele has been demonstrated not through the progressive development of standard plot elements, but through the analysis of the inner conflicts that she undergoes at every little twist and turn in her situation. This is the essence of the novel of personal sensibility, and Miss Stein demonstrates that she has learned her lessons well.

Book Three is subtitled "Helen" and begins with a passionate homily by the narrator on the subject of homesickness. "There is no passion more dominant and instinctive in the human spirit than the need of the country to which one belongs." (53) The little sermon turns in the following paragraph into a fully sensual, impressionistic rendering of London in winter, well worth quoting to show the gift for conventional description that Gertrude Stein almost from the very beginning chose to "subtract" from her art.

An American in the winter fogs of London can realize this passionate need, this desperate longing in all its completeness. The dead weight of that fog and smoke laden air, the sky that never suggests for a moment the clean blue distance that has been the accustomed daily comrade, the dreary sun, moon and stars that look like painted imitations on the ceiling of a smoke-filled room, the soggy, damp, miserable streets, and the women with bedraggled, frayed-out skirts, their faces swollen and pimply with sordid dirt ground into them until it has become a natural part of their ugly surface all become day after day a more dreary weight of hopeless oppression.

It is a passage whose lushness of physical detail would have satisfied an impassioned D. H. Lawrence, though its tone seems out of keeping with the rest of the book. Its effects are too calculated to contrast well with the more stark, analytic passages that predominate.

From the morass of homesickness, Adele steps from the steamer on to the streets of New York. Her return is unexpected, and after six months' absence there is no one to meet her when she disembarks. As she explains to Helen, it is to America more than anything else that she has returned, rejoicing " 'in the New York streets, in the long spindling legs of the elevated, in the straight high undecorated houses, in the empty upper air and in the white surface of the snow.' " (54)

At first, the relationship between Helen and Adele is a bit strained, but after a while the closeness returns and surpasses anything they have had before, and "they agreed between them that they were very near the state of perfect happiness." (55) " 'Yes I guess it's alright,' " Adele answers with her characteristic reticence. She is then aroused from her euphoria "by a kiss that seemed to scale the very walls of chastity." (56) Adele turns from Helen with revulsion and buries her face in her hands. Helen is of course stunned. Adele apologizes, but Helen is inconsolable. " 'Was it that you felt your old distrust of me again?' 'Yes,' replied Adele briefly. 'I am afraid I can't forgive this,' Helen said. 'I didn't suppose that you could,' Adele replied."

They go on seeing one another, and they analyze what they feel to be Adele's problems in taking part in the relationship without inhibitions. Gradually, although their happy relations are once more resumed, a new strain comes about within the relationship. Adele can not go at the same speed as Helen, and Helen demands responses of Adele before she is ready. Knowing Helen's inability to bear rejection, Adele "went farther than she could in honesty because she was unable to refuse anything to one who had given all." (58) The old openness is now impossible. A petty incident upsets Helen. She has been kept waiting in a restaurant and a man has approached her. Adele loses patience with Helen, but Helen, after a dream in which she thinks that Adele has left, capitulates completely and is put in the dependent position. Another quarrel follows in which Adele once again turns on Helen with the accusation: " 'You have no right to constantly use your pain as a weapon!' " (60) They give in to one another once again, "but they both realised that neither of them had yielded." (61)

The relationship takes another turn. Helen has thrown the burden of choice on Adele, and it is now up to Adele to request the next meeting between the two. "Helen's attitude became that of one anxious to give all but unfortunately prevented by time and circumstances." Adele feels that her own greater commitment to the relationship is being taken advantage of, and she rebels, accusing Helen once again of arrogance, facing Helen's familiar counter-accusation of emotional and instinctive coldness. At the crucial moment Adele once again wavers at the door before returning to take Helen in her arms.

As usual, however, the reconciliation has no lasting and improving effect on the relationship. "Helen still pursued her method of granting in inverse ratio [note the mathematical language] to the strength of Adele's desire, and Adele's unhappiness and inward resistance

grew steadily with the increase of her affection."(64)
One day Helen announces that she is going abroad with
Sophie the following summer. The spectre of Sophie
once again rises to cloud the relationship, and Helen
admits that if faced with a choice she would give up
Adele, because Sophie would not be strong enough to
bear it and Adele would. Adele realizes that it is Sophie's
money that is taking Helen to Europe. In the last month
before the departure for Europe the openness of the relationship almost disappears, and Adele and Helen are
under an almost impossible strain, during which the
roles change subtly. Helen is now "irritating and unsat-
isfying, Adele patient and forbearing."(66) The seemingly final rupture comes when Helen breaks a luncheon
engagement with Adele. The bitter feelings rise to a
head, and Adele writes Helen a letter breaking off the
relationship, to which she receives no response.

A few days go by, and Adele is happy that the pres-
sure of the relationship is gone. Then one day she sees
Helen walking in the street, and she is overcome with
affection. She writes to her, professing affection and
offering to receive Helen once again. Helen accepts and
pays Adele a visit. The reconciliation is slow and painful,
and it finally comes about with even less openness remaining than before. "Adele had learned to love and
Helen to trust but still there was no real peace between
them."(68) After a few more minor difficulties they
leave for Europe (Helen once again with Sophie), and
they arrange to meet later that summer in Italy.

They meet in Rome, and Helen confides to Adele that
things are not going well with her and Sophie. The three
of them travel together with pretended friendliness and

spontaneity. Sophie begins to perceive from the actions and demeanor of Helen and Adele the extent of the affection between the two of them, and she begins for the very first time actively to resent the presence of Adele. Helen tells Adele in a moment alone of Sophie's ever-increasing jealousy, not only of Adele but of anyone in whom Helen shows the slightest interest. It falls to Adele to soothe Sophie's feelings constantly, a job she resents. Her still intense affection for Helen is counter-balanced by her growing realization of Helen's penchant for using people and her selling herself to Sophie. " 'What a condemned little prostitute it is,' " Adele comments on Helen to herself. " 'I know there is no use in asking for an explanation. Like Kate Croy she would tell me "I shall sacrifice nothing and nobody" and that's just her situation she wants and will try for everything. . . .' " (75) She is willing to continue simply out of her affection for Helen, and she also professes an analytical interest in the twistings and turnings of the situation. " 'I certainly get very much interested in the mere working of the machinery.' " Helen and Adele are reduced to expressing their love in quiet and secret moments when Sophie is not around, but Sophie is getting more and more perceptive. One day she decrees that she and Helen will leave Rome the following morning.

Before they part, Helen and Adele repledge their affection in guarded words. Adele asks if she must give herself so much to Sophie, but Helen is unable to make any reply. They part on that note, with Adele alone in Rome.

After a few weeks Adele writes to Sophie, forewarning them of the exact times she plans to be in Florence and

Siena so that they can avoid her if they choose to do so. She meets them almost by accident in a restaurant, and they resume the depressing triangle once again. Adele realizes now that she has lost almost all control over Helen and that Sophie is now the dominant force. Helen's will has been reduced to almost nothing. One night they kiss indiscreetly under a light, and Sophie sees them. This adds another complication. Adele's sick depression over Helen's "prostitution" becomes more and more evident. The afternoon before Adele's departure from Florence, Adele and Helen have another final irresolute scene replete with self-doubts and recriminations. The relationship has reached its lowest ebb.

Adele goes for a walking trip with a friend through the Tuscan hills, happy and free, but knowing that when the three of them meet once again in Siena the same unhappiness will begin all over again. The situation when they meet in Siena reflects Adele's forebodings. Adele finally feels that she must confront Helen directly with her feelings about the compromising position in which she has placed herself with Sophie. Helen's answers are completely evasive and inadequate, and Adele in anger avoids her for four days. She realizes now that Sophie is uppermost in Helen's mind. Helen, however, seeks out Adele, and a partial reconciliation takes place.

With the strain between Helen and Adele so obvious, Sophie is now content to reduce her surveillance and permit them more time to be alone. Adele understands now that after Sophie had seen them kissing in Florence, she exacted a promise from Helen not to show any affection to Adele. And so, even their moments alone together are no longer satisfactory in any way, punctuated by long periods of uncomfortable silence. Their final parting is as the others have been, strained and irresolute.

For many weeks after that Adele receives no communication at all from Helen. After many battles with herself, she finally swallows her pride and writes Helen an impassioned, and yet pathetic, letter asking her never to deny that she cares for her and wishing that she had more influence over her. Helen answers by saying that such conditions as she has patiently endured all summer will certainly never arise again. Adele now understands that Helen is still, and obviously always will be, unable to admit that she is uncontrollably bound to Sophie, and that she has sacrificed her freedom by not facing things openly. " 'Can't she see things as they are and not as she would make them if she were strong enough as she plainly isn't.' " (87) She now realizes that the game is over and lost. " 'I am afraid it comes very near being a dead-lock,' she groaned dropping her head on her arms," (88) as the book closes.

A deadlock it is indeed in a number of ways. First of all, from Adele's point of view her attempted relationship with Helen has reached an impasse that looks like a permanent stalemate. Secondly, the plot, which has consisted of a few trips to Europe, and a few get-togethers in New York and Baltimore over a period of about three years, has ended at about the same point at which it began—Sophie is dominant over Helen, and Adele is the outsider looking in. Not only has the plot-line been circular, but its development has not been at all steady in the artificial way common to the working out of the story-line in the average novel of the period. At the moments when we think that the story is taking a rise in develop-

ment there is always a regression in the behavior of
someone to set the development back. As a result, the
complications are mainly interior; that is, within the
consciousness of the individual or within the relationship
of two individuals, rather than complications of circum-
stance which control character. Neither Helen nor Adele
regard their relationship as established at any time during the novel. It is always in progress. They speak as
though it were still something out in front of them that
they were trying to earn, and, for reasons of character
that they have not yet been able to overcome, they have
been unsuccessful in achieving. *Things as They Are* is
the study of the *process* of individual growth and of the
relationships between individuals, and basic to its assumptions about character is that the individual is not a
static mechanism and that the study of a relationship is
not the comparison of similar and divergent qualities of
a number of static mechanisms, but of the interaction of
more than one human consciousness. Character to Gertrude Stein is determined almost exclusively by con-
siousness, and she is inclined to exclude the unconscious
as a factor in the development of personality. This makes
her characters abstractions of a sort which represents
types characterized almost purely by their verbalizations
of themselves. Although the first translations of Freud
were then appearing, Gertrude Stein seems not to have
been influenced at all by him, and she adopted a kind of
Jamesian psychology of consciousness which she kept
basic to her writing throughout the rest of her life. This
kind of character definition by verbalization is not dependent on having educated characters like the young
"emancipated" women in *Things as They Are*. Even the

semiliterate characters of *Three Lives* characterize themselves almost exclusively by the tortuous verbalization of their conscious minds.

Allied with her concepts of consciousness, Gertrude Stein exhibits a kind of determinism that furnishes an interesting comparison to the philosophical naturalistic determinism of Theodore Dreiser. Almost from the very beginning we are aware, in *Things as They Are,* that neither Helen nor Adele has a chance to break from whatever bonds are constraining them into the kind of relationship that both of them seem to want. The deterministic shackles that bind them are as stiff and unbending as those that bind Dreiser's first heroine, but they spring from radically different sources. Carrie Meeber's ultimate unhappiness is the result of the circumstances of her birth and her ascension through a society that permits the "tough" individual to survive and rise, but permits him victory in only a circumstantial sense, and not in terms of individual self-fulfillment. The fatal forces are external to the individual, and all one can do to survive is to be one of the "fittest," and to play the game demanded of him. But with the characters of Gertrude Stein the seeds of each individual's fate lie not without but within the individual consciousness. And this fate is not something one can escape. It is a part of the very bottom nature of the individual, and he can no more change it than he can exchange one of his limbs for another. She was to say at the beginning of *The Making of Americans,* her most elaborate study of character, "It is hard living down the tempers we are born with."[6] This is basic to all her writings about people. Dreiser's

6 Gertrude Stein, *The Making of Americans* (Paris, 1925), p. 3.

socially-determined and inexorable hand of fate has almost no existence in her work. The consciousness and character of the individual are all.[7]

It is easy to see from the long summary of *Things as They Are* what Gertrude Stein's attitude is toward the portrayal of reality and realistic verisimilitude. For one thing, Miss Stein's portrayal of reality employs a different kind of selection from that of most of the so-called "realists." Her realist contemporaries were for the most part interested in telling the life story, or a substantial part of it, of the main character of the novel, replete with much detail and a more or less loose organization of incidents. The existence of an organizing theme in the book becomes evident after the piling up of detail begins to show a trend in a certain direction. The traditional realist, of course, did not include everything in the fabric of the life of his character, for that would have been impossible; but the incidents and details that he selected ranged widely throughout his subjects, and were not limited to a necessarily direct connection with thematic material.

Gertrude Stein's technique differs radically. For one thing, it is more that of the short story writer. She develops a single theme immediately and dwells on it to the exclusion of almost everything else. The detail, conversation, and incident that appear in *Things as They Are*

[7] John Malcolm Brinnin also sees these attributes as all-important to Miss Stein's development of character, *The Third Rose*, p. 59:

> Her situations are devised less for dramatic action and eventful continuity than for opportunities to observe character as a type of consciousness. The world Gertrude Stein's characters inhabit is strictly limited to the range of their personalities and their intellectual capacities.

are focused unremittingly on the development of the triangle. We know almost nothing about the girls that lies outside the context of their relationship to one another. Background deatil is scrupulously avoided. For all we know, none of the women has had a childhood with the exception of Helen, about whom we are told one incident from her past as an illustration of a personality trait that has a direct bearing on her relationship with both Sophie and Adele. Miss Stein has abstracted from the complexities of her characters' lives the one theme of their interrelationship and has subordinated everything in the narrative to the illumination of this theme. Within this context, however, her selectivity does not have the same kind of concision. She throws in *everything* that relates to her theme, tortuous arguments, lovers' quarrels, trips, and visits, over and over again to express the essentially repetitive quality of life as she sees it. Life to Gertrude Stein is not a convenient package with a beginning, middle, and end as it was for the conventional novelists. It consists of all the tedious monotony of most everyday existences and of repetition not only of boring habit, but also of events whose character is dictated by the basic nature of the individual. And yet, although the events of *Things as They Are* seem on the surface to have a monotonous sameness, each of the events occurs at a more complex stage of the relationship and adds to its complexity. Thus, within the surface sameness of the elements of the novel, each of the events has its own uniqueness within the context of the relationship. By abstracting from the lives of three women only that part of their complex characters that relates them to one another and by subjecting their consciousness and the tedious repetitions of their lives that their consciousness determines to the ruthless analysis of her literary microscope, Gertrude Stein is able to express on the page her view of the complexity of life and of the individual consciousness. The microscopic world-view and analytic point of view remain basic to Gertrude Stein's methodology throughout her long career as a writer of English.

The sense of realistic verisimilitude in *Things as They Are* is also very much affected by the analytic methodology of its author. Gertrude Stein is only rarely interested in "rendering" action. In her penchant for analysis she describes some events, tells about others, renders a few, and lets her characters discuss either within their own consciousness or with one another things that have happened, changes that have taken place. She spends little or no time setting the scene or showing the small movements of her characters to give the reader a sense of their genuine physical presence or movement. The characters of *Things as They Are* are objects of analysis rather than "real" people in the traditional realistic sense. Their problems engage sympathy, but it is a mind with which we are involved, a human consciousness rather than a "rounded" individual. This abstract sense of what composes people becomes even more prevalent in her later and more analytic works. The individual consciousness will disappear even further until it is lost completely in a general "type."

It would seem from the above discussion, then, that Gertrude Stein was wiser in her choice of a title than were her posthumous editors. *Quod Erat Demonstrandum* (which, roughly translated, means "which was to be demonstrated") gives a real sense of the geometric exactitude with which Gertrude Stein has dissected her objects of study. In many ways, *Things as They Are* is the demonstration of a proof of certain theorems on the subject of personality. It is more than that, of course, but Gertrude Stein's choice of *Quod Erat Demonstrandum* as a title gives somewhat of a clue as to the nature of her intentions, which seem adequately born out by the work itself. *Things as They Are* shows a careful structural balance around the theme of the triangle. There are three books within the novelette, each bearing the name of one of the sides of the triangle. There are three trips to Europe. There is a balance among the three personalities present within the triangle. The slow-moving and sensual Adele is played off against the prudish and calculating Sophie. Both are striving to cement the affection of the passionate and headstrong Helen (the hypotenuse, if you will). Three years is the length of time that elapses in the story, with the second year the high point of the relationship between Adele and Helen. And so on. It is not worth pushing the point, except to show that Gertrude Stein's obvious concern with the geometric balance of *Things as They Are* adds still another abstract element to the ones enumerated before.

As for matters of grammer, vocabulary, and syntax, *Things as They Are* shows little that is unconventional except for a tendency to run sentences together without punctuation or with only a comma separating them. The tyranny of the present participle does not come about in her work until *Three Lives*. Miss Stein is as yet content with the conventional use of nouns, and is not interested in replacing them with participles or gerunds. Her doctrine of the continuous present, as reflected in her use of present participles, does not achieve any systematic formal existence until "Melanctha." It is not prefigured in *Things as They Are.*

In her mature style, Gertrude Stein is often in the habit of reflecting the kind of action or tension present in her story by repeating certain key words over and over again in the same context to give the emotion a stylized formalization. The same characteristic is present in *Things as They Are,* although not to the point of stylization. The story is told from the point of view of Adele's consciousness, and it is primarily concerned with her struggle to achieve the kind of friendship she desires with Helen Thomas. When the problems created by this attempt at friendship are uppermost in Adele's mind the characteristic words that appear are "struggle," "resentment," "pain," "reluctance," "protest," "quarrel," "submission," and "bitterness." This use of words has not been at this point stylized to the point of conscious abstractionism, but this is a trait of Gertrude Stein's later style that is evident even now.

There is also not yet any consistent violation of syntax in *Things as They Are.* Miss Stein always stays within the generally standard sentence structure of subject-verb-object and its variants. She violates syntax later in her work by doing away with connectives, either in terms of related thoughts or in terms of correlative conjunctions, and by re-ordering sentences. None of this takes place here, however. Her paragraphs are organic units for the most part, with an obvious relationship running throughout all the sentences from first to last. There is no indication here that there will be any change from this style in any of her later writings.

The one element of style in which there is the most

obvious use of an idiosyncratic characteristic that is to play a major role in her later stylistic abstractionism is punctuation. From the quotes included in the text of this chapter it is obvious that her punctuational patterns do not match those of traditional grammar. It is difficult, however, to determine how much of this is due to conscious abstractionism. Miss Stein did not see *Things as They Are* through the press. A lot of the idiosyncratic punctuation may merely be the product of an unrevised first draft. A lot of it may also be due to Miss Stein's weak sense of the traditional punctuation. In Miss Stein's later writing the absence of commas and certain connectives is the working out of a consciously articulated doctrine to engage the reader actively in the creative process by forcing him to understand and analyze the texture of the sentence he is reading. It is a disorientative process, similar to others we shall discuss in later chapters. A traditional punctuational pattern is promised and then violated. This conscious use of idiosyncratic punctuation does not seem to be as obvious in the case of *Things as They Are.*

The distinction between what is conscious and what is accidental on the part of an author is at best a tenuous process. In this instance, however, we are fortunate in having Gertrude Stein's Radcliffe themes as a document for comparison. In a context in which she was to be penalized for faulty punctuation and grammar, Gertrude Stein would more than likely have attempted to conform as closely to the traditional forms as she was capable of doing. If her sense of standard grammar and punctuation was weak at this time, then we may probably assume that it had not gotten stronger in the years she spent away from any kind of formal discipline in this direction.

I have chosen two selections from among the many themes that Gertrude Stein wrote while taking English Composition 22 under William Vaughn Moody. In the second theme that Gertrude Stein wrote at Radcliffe (Nov. 7, 1894) the following constitutes the first half of the opening paragraph:

> Two girls strolled into the park one summer day and threw themselves on the grass: one full on her back, the other raised herself on her elbow and as if continuing a conversation said, "Yes I fully understand your feeling toward my father. He is moody bitter and often tyrannical at home; we all recognize that but poor old dad we love him anyway. Wait I'll tell you a little of his life, its only just that you should know it."[8]

The differences between Gertrude Stein's punctuation here and the more standard variety are obvious. She has very little idea where to place commas, her phrasing is awkward, and her sense of the structure of the English sentence is weak. The instructor has marked the phrase following the colon after "grass," the absence of a comma after "moody," the semi-colon after "home," the absence of a comma after "Wait," and the missing apostrophe of "its." Throughout all of the early compositions Miss Stein continually brings down the wrath of Mr. Moody and her instructors for the awkwardness of her phrasing and her "disdain for the more necessary marks of punctuation," (126) although there is occasional grudging praise for her "vividness and imaginative

[8] Rosalind S. Miller, *Gertrude Stein: Form and Intelligibility* (New York, 1949), p. 111. From now on, numbers in the text refer to this edition.

force." (109) Her sense of style and grace is still in obvious need of training.

By the end of her freshman year she is capable in her final theme (May 22, 1895) of sentences such as the following:

> She seemed to herself, to be growing apathetic. She tried to force herself to move but she could not. She upbraided herself, she grew more violent in her thoughts and yet she did not move. (155)

Aside from the obvious balance of the sentences, there is powerful use of repetition of the word "she" to make emphatic the violent state of mind of her character. There still remains, however, the disinclination or inability to use commas properly enough to satisfy traditional grammar. The reappearance of the characteristics of repetition and idiosyncratic punctuation eight years later in *Things as They Are* shows that they were a part of Gertrude Stein's characteristic writing from the very beginning and became a highly conscious part of her later abstractionism.

To judge from the above that Miss Stein has merely elevated her inability to use the traditional forms of English punctuation into a doctrine of writing is to speak evaluatively, which I have earlier disavowed. It is my purpose mainly to point out that these elements appear in her writing from the very beginning. If indeed she capitalized on her weaknesses and turned them into a later important characteristic of her style, it is no more or less than many other artists have done. That the supposedly "faulty" use of grammar later becomes a very *conscious* part of her abstract style is amply documented by the essay "Poetry and Grammar" in *Lectures in America*,[9] as well as by her creative writings themselves.

I have endeavored in this chapter to show that although *Things as They Are* is not a genuinely abstract piece of writing, it nonetheless prefigures many of the abstract elements that are to appear in her more characteristic performances. It is now time to turn from the mere hints of abstractionism to its more full-bodied appearance in Miss Stein's next work, *Three Lives*.

---

[9] Boston, 1957.

3
Three Lives

AFTER FINISHING *Things as They Are*, GERTRUDE STEIN turned to the translation of one of Gustave Flaubert's final works, *Trois Contes*. Sitting in her study beneath Cézanne's "La Femme au Chapeau," she began to render into English the *mots justes* of the great French master of style. The juxtaposition of Cézanne and Flaubert when viewed in retrospect must surely appear symbolic, because from each Miss Stein seems to have learned a lesson that profoundly influenced her art. From Flaubert she learned that the carefully molded style was the most important instrument in the art of the writer of fiction, a lesson also learned well by her contemporary, James Joyce. From Cézanne she seems to have learned that the depiction of external reality does not depend on the amount of detail included, but can be accomplished by abstracting from the welter of detail that appears to the senses the repetitive properties that constitute the

sine qua non of the external object. For Cézanne this
sine qua non consisted of the basic geometric pattern
underlying each physical object. For Gertrude Stein the
configuration is composed of the basic attributes that she
feels make up the personality whose portrait she is creating, mainly through the conscious manifestations of personality traits. We have seen the original tendencies in
this direction in *Things as They Are*. In *Three Lives*,
especially in "Melanctha," Gertrude Stein uses the carefully and consciously wrought style to create her abstract conceptions of personality types. This is the real
beginning of her abstract style.

Three Lives followed immediately upon the translation of Flaubert.[1] It would seem that Gertrude Stein was
influenced significantly by only one of the *Trois Contes*,[2]
"Un Coeur Simple," the story of "a simple heart" who
throughout her entire life was the devoted servant of a
moderately wealthy woman of the upper middle class.
The story proceeds in episodic fashion to present the
reader with the events of Felicité's life and the characteristics of her personality. Flaubert does not delve into
the unconscious of his character, as he does with Emma
Bovary, but rather presents the reader with descriptions
of her personality traits and selected occurrences chosen
from the course of her entire life. No incident is developed in elaborate detail or given major significance except as a part of the total picture of Felicité. If there are

[1] Unfortunately, no traces of this translation exist among the pa-
pers of the Gertrude Stein Collection at the Yale Collection of
American Literature.

[2] A good translation of this work by Arthur McDowall was published by New Directions (New York, 1947), with an introduction by
Harry Levin.

implications to be drawn as to what lies beneath the conscious exterior of Flaubert's character, it is up to the reader to draw them.

The technique of "The Good Anna" and "The Gentle Lena" is very similar in the above respects to that of Flaubert. In addition, the subject matter of each parallels to a marked degree the story of "Un Coeur Simple." The main figure in each story is a servant girl who works for a wealthy middle class woman. None of the individual events of their lives is more important than any other. Neither of the women has aspirations that rise above those appropriate to her class in society. There is no "story," as in Flaubert's tale, only an attempt at a total picture of a human consciousness. The relationship of Gertrude Stein to Flaubert is the subject for another study. It is important here to notice it merely as a germinal stage in the development of Gertrude Stein's first genuine step into abstractionism.

Some of the nascent elements of Gertrude Stein's abstract style are evident on the first page of "The Good Anna."

> Anna managed the *whole little house* for Miss Mathilda. It was a *funny little house* . . . They were *funny little houses,* two stories high, with red brick fronts and long white steps.
>
> This *one little house* was always very full with Miss Mathilda, an under servant, stray dogs and cats and Anna's voice that *scolded, managed, grumbled* all day long.[3] (Italics mine)

The first four italicized phrases are examples of one of Miss Stein's earliest uses of repetition. Here the effect is

[3] *Three Lives* (New York, 1936), p. 11. All page references in the text refer to this edition. We shall follow the same procedure as in the previous chapter throughout the book.

little more than an emphasizing of the phrase *little house* with a few variations on the preceding modifier. The technique is picked up and then dropped immediately, giving the impression of being almost unconsciously used by the author. It is not yet a conscious part of Miss Stein's style, but as *Three Lives* progresses it is used with more and more frequency, especially in description of people. On page 17 there is a description of the servant Katy who comes with Anna to work for Miss Mathilda. The narrator refers to her "peasant english [*sic*]" and her "servile humor" and states that "old Katy was too coarsely made from natural earth for that." The narrator finally refers to Katy as a "rough old creature." In the following paragraph Miss Stein repeats these various characteristics in a sentence that sums up Katy for us as seen through the eyes of Anna: "An earthy, uncouth, servile peasant creature old Katy surely was."

The last italicized phrase of the paragraphs quoted above is another example of the summing-up sentence, a device that Gertrude Stein employs throughout *Three Lives*. Here it is used to sum up the typical day in the servant life of the Good Anna, a day in which she "scolded, managed, grumbled." In the preceding example the summing-up sentence was used to repeat the characteristics of one of the characters and to establish her personality for all time. Still another use of the summing-up sentence is to introduce one of the characters into the story:

Mrs. Lehntman was a good looking woman. She had a plump well rounded body, clear olive skin, bright dark eyes and crisp black curling hair. She was pleasant, magnetic, efficient and good. She was very attractive, very generous and very amiable.(30)

Such descriptions add to the abstractionism of the story by stating rather than rendering (in the Jamesian sense). Gertrude Stein feels no need to attempt the illusion of verisimilitude through a presentation of Mrs. Lehntman in various situations that demonstrate her pleasantness, attractiveness, generosity, and amiability. Having made these statements about Mrs. Lehntman, Gertrude Stein then assumes that the reader has accepted these qualities as a part of her character's personality. The abstracting of these characteristics renders the portrait of Mrs. Lehntman an abstraction. Mrs. Lehntman is a solid figure composed of permanent and enduring qualities, much the same as the figures in a Cézanne portrait. There is no attempt on the part of Gertrude Stein to give this character or any of the characters in "The Good Anna" the illusion of movement in a specific physical environment.

There are a number of uses of repetition in "The Good Anna" and "The Gentle Lena" other than the types we have just discussed. In the latter story a single word is occasionally used repetitively to emphasize a particular characteristic in the physical description of a character.

Lena was a brown and pleasant creature, brown as blonde races often have them brown, brown, not with the yellow or the red or the chocolate brown of sun burned countries, but brown with the clear color laid flat on the light toned skin beneath, the plain, spare brown that makes it right to have been made with hazel eyes, and not too abundant straight, brown hair, hair that only later deepens itself into brown from the straw yellow of a german childhood. (240)

"Brown," when used as above, becomes a solid and recurrent quality rather than merely a color, and as a quality it is an element of abstraction. Also, however, we must never overlook the simple characteristic of word play, a characteristic that will become more and more dominant in the writing of Gertrude Stein.

Another use of repetition is in the description of inner physical condition:

> Lena was very sick on the voyage. She thought, surely before it was over that she would die. She was so sick she could not even wish that she had not started. She could not eat, she could not moan, she was just blank and scared, and sure that every minute she would die. She could not hold herself in, nor help herself in her trouble. She just staid where she had been put, pale, and scared, and weak, and sick, and sure that she was going to die. (246)

Through repetition, the sense of Lena's sickness is emphatically presented, even though we do not suffer along with her as we would have in a "realistic" novel, where with detailed immediacy her discomfort would have been rendered.

Another type of repetition is the use of the same opening clause in neighboring sentences. On page 264 the following two sentences open the first and third paragraphs:

> Herman's married sister liked her brother Herman, and she had always tried to help him, when there was anything she knew he wanted.

> Herman's married sister liked her brother Herman, and she did not want him not to like to be with women.

This is the type of repetition for which Gertrude Stein has achieved a special kind of notoriety, especially in her early portraits of Matisse and Picasso, and which she elevated into an almost philosophical doctrine in *The Making of Americans.* Each character at all times keeps certain characteristics permanent and unchanging. Within this permanence of quality, there are possibilities for a variety of actions and responses consistent with the permanent qualities. Herman's married sister always liked Herman, but within this there is room for a variety of other actions and responses. We see here Gertrude Stein's characteristic repetition at its primitive inception.

The emphasis on personality, class, and racial types, a concern that is to be most important to *The Making of Americans,* makes its appearance in "The Good Anna" and "The Gentle Lena," and is evident in many of the descriptions.

Lena had the flat chest, straight back and forward falling shoulders of the patient and enduring working woman, though her body was now still in its milder girlhood and work had not yet made these lines too clear. (240)

Lena is the working-class type.

The Good Anna is always conscious of her station in life, and particularly of the peculiar kind of "ugliness" appropriate to the dress of each of the classes. She "always found new people to befriend, people who, *in the kindly fashion of the poor,* used up her savings and then gave promises in place of payments."(65, italics mine) For Gertrude Stein there are typical physical developments or actions that have a direct relation to the class structure. It is another instance of her attempt to abstract permanent qualities she feels are inherent in particular conceptual groups.

In the same vein we see the emphasis on a kind of racial or national type:

> There was no fever in this friendship, it was just the interchange of two hard working, worrying women, the one large and motherly, with the pleasant, patient, soft, worn, tolerant face that comes with a german husband to obey ... (45-6)

> The old Kreders were to an Irish nature, a stingy, dirty couple. They had not the free-hearted, thoughtless, fighting, mud bespattered, ragged, peat-smoked cabin dirt that Irish Mary knew and could forgive and love. Theirs was the german dirt of saving, of being dowdy and loose and foul in your clothes so as to save them and yourself in washing ... (268)

There are obviously types of behavior indigenous to each nationality.

Finally, there are types of personality that simply exist with no necessary psychologically determined patterns of behavior:

> Herman Kreder was cleaner than the old people, just because it was his nature to keep cleaner, but he was used to his mother and his father, and he never thought that they should keep things cleaner. (269)

> Mrs. Drehten was a mild, worn, unaggressive nature that never cared to influence or to lead. (69)

These personality types are to take over in *The Making of Americans,* as "attacking" and "resisting" and "yielding" types work their wills on one another. The type is more real in many instances to Gertrude Stein than the individual, because the nature of the individual's behavior, thought, and emotions is always determined by the class of personality, national, or social types to which he belongs. Gertrude Stein's psychological determinism goes first from the class to the individual, rather than the other way. The abstracting of various types of character is still another example of the growing abstractionism that we are witnessing in *Three Lives*.

The narrative structure of both "The Good Anna" and "The Gentle Lena" is episodic in the same way as Flaubert's "Un Coeur Simple." We are presented with a character, told something about her present, told something about her past, meet a few of her relatives and acquaintances, see her perform in a few quickly developed situations, and follow her to the grave. The internal development of the characters is not dynamic. As in *Things as They Are,* we are given a proposition about a particular type of personality and then a series of demonstrations of the proposition. "The Gentle Lena" opens with the following paragraph: "Lena was patient, gentle, sweet and german. She had been a servant for four years and had liked it very well." (239) Except for the fact of her simplemindedness (which is at least implied in the opening statement), there is almost nothing else about Lena's personality that we learn throughout the rest of the narrative.

The following statements sum up just about all there is to know about the essential personality of the Good Anna: "Anna was a medium sized, thin, hard working, worrying woman" (31); "our good Anna with her spinster body, her firm jaw, her humorous, light, clean eyes and her lined, worn, thin, pale yellow face." (46)

It is the essential attributes of her characters as she sees them that are of interest to Gertrude Stein. The lives of Lena and Anna are merely concrete demonstrations of the abstract qualities that make up each of their personalities. The unconscious forces or yearnings that lie within Anna or Lena are never articulated by either Gertrude Stein or the characters themselves. The actions of the characters tell us nothing significant about them that Gertrude Stein does not tell us at some time herself. If the characters happen to live in our memories, they are more rock-like examples of qualities in the human consciousness of various types than flesh-and-blood people who suffer, yearn, and love.

One of the problems is that Gertrude Stein is attempting to give expression to almost totally inarticulate people. Indeed, Lena is so inarticulate that she is incapable of expressing even her likes and dislikes. However, we have seen previously that the almost monstrously verbal figures in *Things as They Are* emerged more as examples of mental consciousness than as living human beings. It is not the education or intelligence quotient of her characters that determine their abstractness, but rather Gertrude Stein's attitude toward them. With the eye of the psychological experimenter Gertrude Stein views her fictional characters as the subjects of a grand experiment in the discovery of the various types of people that exist in the world, as demonstrated through the conscious articulation or manifestation of personality in action or thought.

The role of the narrator changes in *Three Lives* from what it was in *Things as They Are*. Instead of the urbane and sophisticated observer who stood above the events of his characters, this narrator envelops himself in a narrative tone that reflects the very dialects of the characters themselves. He not only reflects the dialect of the characters, but he expresses the inarticulate thoughts of the characters in the very language that they would use were they able to express their thoughts for themselves. The narrator thus becomes as important as any character in the story, not merely as the functional agent who relates the events of the narrative, but as the consciousness that expresses the inarticulate thoughts of the simple figures that people the tale. On the stylistic level the narrator accomplishes this by affecting a simplicity of diction and an occasional stilting of the syntax to sound like the speech of immigrants. This is most evident when the narrator is expressing ideas close to the consciousness of Anna or Lena rather than when he is describing something not directly related to either.

> She watched and scolded hard these days to make young Julia do the way she should. Not that Julia Lehntman was pleasant in the good Anna's sight, but it must never be that a young girl growing up should have no one to make her learn to do things right.(39)

> And so when any day one might need life and help from others of the working poor, there was no way a woman who had a little saved could say them no.(65)

This, too, is a narrator who, like his counterpart in *Things as They Are,* is perfectly willing to inject his own comments into the story.

> But, alas this world of ours is after all much what it should be and cheerful Miss Mathilda had her troubles too with Anna. (22)

The tone of the narrator even in the comment is consistent with the narrator's tone throughout.

The seemingly faulty grammar and punctuation which were noticeable in *Things as They Are* are almost totally unobtrusive, even though they are still present. In *Three*

Lives, however, they seem very much in keeping with the narrative tone that projects the immigrant English onto the page. It is here also for the first time that we see Gertrude Stein's life-long habit of dropping the capital letters at the beginning of the adjective forms of the names of nationalities. Both of these characteristics are an aid to the narrative tone as a reflection through the narrator of the educational level of the characters.

We see also for the first time the earliest beginnings of Gertrude Stein's use of the present participle as a substantive:

"Why you stand there so stupid, why don't you answer, Lena," said Mrs. Haydon one Sunday, at the end of a long *talking* that she was giving Lena about Herman Kreder . . . (252, italics mine)

" . . . but that was no good that *marrying* for that poor Lena, Mrs. Aldrich." (274, italics mine)

The few instances of this use of the present participle in "The Good Anna" and "The Gentle Lena" are a small prefiguring of the sudden explosion of substantive present participles that takes place in "Melanctha" and remains an integral part of Gertrude Stein's abstract style throughout the rest of her work.

The three stories of *Three Lives* are perhaps more important for their differences than their similarities, but it will be valuable first to take a quick look at the latter. They are all set in the town of Bridgepoint, almost totally unlocalized in "The Good Anna" and "The Gentle Lena" except by being placed in the South, which Gertrude Stein chooses to capitalize. All the subjects of the tales are from the servant class. The stories follow their main characters throughout their lives to the grave. The deaths are in no way climactic, but rather occur in a minor key that serves to put a simple period to the story. The tales show the same attempt on the part of the narrator to simulate the dialect of the various characters in a kind of primitive stream of consciousness. All three are told in the same kind of episodic pattern that avoids the artificial continuity of events lying at the heart of every "realistic" novel. The central characters are "inarticulate" to a more or less marked degree. It is possible to go on making this kind of comparison. However, it is more important to turn to the differences between "Melanctha" and the other two tales to show how big a step Gertrude Stein takes into abstractionism.

"Melanctha" goes farther toward abstractionism than its sister stories in a number of ways. The first extension is in its scope. As we have discussed before, "The Good Anna" and "The Gentle Lena" are largely demonstrations of propositions about various personality types. Their scope goes very little beyond this. The demonstrations are worked out with exceeding care, but relations between characters are not developed beyond the mere statement that a relationship exists. These characteristics have been pointed out before by Donald Sutherland: "Where 'The Good Anna' and 'The Gentle Lena' are composed as the presentation of a single type in illustrative incidents, 'Melanctha' is composed on the dramatic trajectory of a passion." And further, "The events considered in 'Melanctha' are mostly the movements of the passion, how Jeff and Melanctha feel differently toward each other from moment to moment."[4] This, of course, is

[4] *Gertrude Stein: A Biography of Her Work* (New Haven, 1951), p. 44.

true as far as it goes. But it fails to take into account a few things. The first is that it is not the "passion" that is all important, but how this passion effects any changes on the characters involved. Also, the moment-to-moment changes in the feelings of Jeff Campbell and Melanctha Herbert toward one another are not important in themselves. It is rather that through the seemingly endless repetitions of similar discussions, internal mental ruminations, arguments, and events (which occur rarely), these changes in feelings occur in subtle, almost imperceptible ways through the cataloguing of effects. The change in attitude of a character is an accomplished state of mind almost before we can notice it. The technique is almost exactly the same as in *Things as They Are*. Every up and down in the relationship of Jeff Campbell and Melanctha is carefully charted, mostly through the thoughts and speeches of each of the characters, and we are able to follow the dynamics of the process of the relationship, which is more dynamic in its development than either of the characters.

"Melanctha" begins in a fashion similar to the other stories in *Three Lives*. The narrative opens with incidents in the present time. After a few pages of episodes in present time Miss Stein shifts us into Melanctha's childhood, in which we see her as a little girl and meet her parents. The union of Melanctha's "big black virile negro" father, "a common, decent enough, colored workman," (90) and her "wandering and mysterious and uncertain" mother sow the psychologically deterministic seeds that create ultimately the "graceful, pale yellow, intelligent, attractive negress" (86) who "wandered, always seeking but never more than very dimly seeing wisdom." (97) We follow her from childhood through adolescence into young womanhood, watching the effects of heredity and the brutalizing presence of her father becoming manifest in the human consciousness known as Melanctha. The structure of "Melanctha" is almost exactly the same as that of "The Good Anna" and "The Gentle Lena." A short opening section introduces us to the main character in present time, after which we shift into the past to learn what events in the background of the character have led to the determination of the present personality. The elaboration of the past life leads us through carefully chosen incidents rather than a continuous narrative into the present once again where a few more incidents are observed, a crisis takes place, and the story trails off to its end. Gertrude Stein is manipulating time, always keeping in mind that the present moment (whether in past, present, or future time) is an accumulation of the moments that have preceded it. Since the traditional temporal sense of narrative fiction is lacking here, there is no climactic note on which any of the stories end. The short final section of each of the tales deals with the summary demise of the heroine. The key is decidedly a minor one, as none of the deaths is the tragic outcome of inevitable circumstances growing out of the character of the heroine, but is simply Miss Stein's way of putting an ending to a story that is basically undramatic in its impact.

Gertrude Stein reinforces her conceptions of time by repeating certain key passages at the beginning of the book and toward the end, when we revert once again to the present. The tale opens with the following statements:

Rose Johnson made it very hard to bring her baby to its birth.

Melanctha Herbert who was Rose Johnson's friend, did everything that any woman could.

The child though it was healthy after it was born, did not live long. Rose Johnson was careless and negligent and selfish, and when Melanctha had to leave for a few days, the baby died. (85)

One hundred forty pages later, after we have returned from the Jeff Campbell episode into the present time of the narrative, the following passages appear:

Rose had a hard time to bring her baby to its birth and Melanctha did everything that any woman could.

The baby though it was healthy after it was born did not live long. Rose Johnson was careless and negligent and selfish and when Melanctha had to leave for a few days the baby died. (224-5)

With a few negligible changes the same words are repeated almost verbatim. The undefined present is yoked over the past to the present that has been developed by the past. By tampering in this way with the standard time continuum of the straightforward, "realistic" narrative, Gertrude Stein has rendered time abstract by turning it into an almost plastic element that can be manipulated at her will. In this sense, the stories of *Three Lives* look forward to other manipulations of time such as *The Waves, Remembrance of Things Past,* and *The Alexandria Quartet.*

The emphasis on the importance of present time is brought home most strongly by the first calculated use of the present participle. As we discussed in connection with *Things as They Are,* Gertrude Stein is most interested in the *process* of relationships. Although her characters usually do not evolve, relationships are always dynamic. One of the startling characteristics of "Melanctha" is the sudden appearance of the present participle as an aid in the sense of process. The very nature of the *ing* ending contains within it the idea of process. To say that something "was beginning" is first of all to place the action in past time. But the action is not merely something that has already taken place. It is an action that during time past is a continuously occurring process. Furthermore, the present participle, even when used as a substantive, retains the idea of process. Jeff and Melanctha rarely talk about their "love"; it is always their "loving." Jeff says that Melanctha is "sweet and thinking," rather than "thoughtful." The effect of the present participle can be seen well in a comparison of almost identical passages from "Melanctha" and *Things as They Are*. Early in the latter book, Adele asks Helen, "Tell me how much do you care for me." Helen's answer is, "Care for you my dear, more than you know and less than you think."[5] In "Melanctha," Jeff demands, "Tell me just straight out how much do you care about me, Miss Melanctha." Her answer: "I certainly do care for you Jeff Campbell less than you are always thinking and much more than you are knowing." (132) The use of present participles changes the meaning of her answer subtly. She is not saying, as Helen did to Adele in the earlier book, that at the present moment she cares for Jeff more than he knows and less than he thinks. What she is saying in this stylized answer is that in the *process* of the relationship the sum of the thoughts and knowledge that

[5] *Things as They Are* (Pawlet, Vt., 1950), p. 15.

are continuously present to Jeff are at variance with the actual state of Melanctha's feelings. It is the continuous present of the *process* of the relationship that Gertrude Stein is emphasizing in this use of the present participle. The analysis of a long passage of descriptive narration will shed further light on Gertrude Stein's use of the present participle:

Jeff sat there this evening in his chair and was silent a long time, *warming* himself with the pleasant fire. He did not look at Melanctha who was *watching*. He sat there and just looked into the fire. At first his dark, open face was *smiling,* and he was *rubbing* the back of his black-brown hand over his mouth to help him in his *smiling.* Then he was *thinking,* and he frowned and rubbed his head hard, to help him in his *thinking.* Then he smiled again, but now his *smiling* was not very pleasant. His smile was now *wavering* on the edge of *scorning.* His smile changed more and more, and then he had a look as if he were deeply down, all disgusted. Now his face was darker, and he was bitter in his *smiling,* and he began, without *looking* from the fire, to talk to Melanctha, who was now very tense with her *watching.* (137, italics mine)

The appearance of this passage occurs at a point when Melanctha has yet to win over the recalcitrantly puritanical Jeff to her way of life. Jeff is constantly wavering between his old middle-class morality and the more casual way of living that is characteristic of Melanctha's habits. When he is with Melanctha he accepts her. Away from her his feelings of guilt torment him. "Jeff always loved now to be with Melanctha and yet he always hated to go to her." (136) The torment is a constant thing with Jeff, so much so that from moment to moment he vacillates between the poles that seem open to him. When he is near Melanctha the torment doubles in intensity, so that almost in successive instants his mood changes. In this passage Gertrude Stein has abstracted a moment of time during which we are able to watch Jeff going through the *process* of mental anguish that is typical behavior for him in the context of this relationship. We see him sitting by the fire, watched by Melanctha. He looks in the fire and smiles. Then he thinks and frowns and rubs his head with his hand. Then he smiles again, but not pleasantly. His smile changes slowly to an expression of disgust, a smile of bitterness, and without looking away from the fire at any time, he begins to talk to Melanctha, "who was now very tense with her watching."

All of this takes place in a few moments of time, and yet so much takes place of importance. How is Gertrude Stein able to capture the feeling of process? The mere listing of the changes in Jeff Campbell's mood would not have been enough. There is something more, and this extra element is the use of the present participle in a unique way. The key verbs in the paragraph almost all end in *ing;* smiling, thinking, wavering, scorning, looking, watching. All the words that most significantly denote the conceptual steps in the process of Jeff Campbell's state of mind end in the grammatical form that linguistically denotes process. This marriage of style and content enables the paragraph to capture not only a present moment of time, but to capture it in the *process* of its being.[6]

On the surface the passage would seem to outdo the realists at their own game. Miss Stein has succeeded in

---

[6] A further note of interest is that this moment occurs in past time in the context of the story.

capturing on paper the illusion of two characters in a tense moment of interaction. And yet, the paragraph must ultimately be seen as abstract in the context of our definition for at least two reasons. First, and least important, the stylistic idiosyncracy of the present participle has the partial effect of slowing down or distorting the ordinary syntactical rhythm we usually associate with standard English. Secondly, Gertrude Stein has abstracted her passage from the larger flow of time of the narrative. She has succeeded in capturing the verisimilitude of a moment, but there is movement of a sort only within the moment. Outside the moment of time itself this incident is simply another accretion in the series of effects that go into the making up of the life of Melanctha Herbert. Within the moment there is a transition from one state of mind to the next. However, this incident in the light of the whole story provides no logical transition, but simply another demonstration of the potentialities of the relationship between personalities. It is a "still point" within which there is movement.

The use of language as an almost plastic element plays an increasing role in "Melanctha," as Gertrude Stein manipulates the word order to change the "tone" of the narrative or to render the general sense of Negro dialect more convincingly. Her main agent for the manipulation of language is her narrator, whose function varies in "Melanctha" even from what it was in the other stories of the book. In this tale the narrator is even more submerged into the narrative tone. His voice rises in pitch and falls according to the character whose actions he is describing or whose thoughts he is recording. He sometimes speaks through the consciousness of a particular character, sometimes in the voice one character would use in describing another, still at other times in a "collective Bridgepoint Negro 'chorus.' "[7] There are times when the narrator speaks an almost ordinary "straightforward" prose:

> Boys had never meant much to Melanctha. They had always been too young to content her. Melanctha had a strong respect for any kind of successful power. (96)

And there are still other times that the narrator intrudes with rhetorical questions almost in the manner of a soap opera:

> What was it that now really happened to them? What was it that Melanctha did, that made everything get all ugly for them? What was it that Melanctha felt then . . .? (155)

This narrator is also quite capable of using almost King James rhythms in describing the anxieties of his characters:

> And now the pain came hard and harder in Jeff Campbell, and he groaned, and it hurt him so, he could not bear it. And the tears came, and his heart beat, and he was hot and worn and bitter in him. (204)

As we can see, one of the characteristics of Gertrude Stein's work beginning to emerge in "Melanctha" is the ability or the propensity to write in a number of different styles even within the same work, a trait she shares with another twentieth-century abstractionist, James Joyce. The style bends to conform with the situation, to control its tone or rhythm. This is another step away from the traditional concept of realistic verisimilitude in which the tone or rhythm of a situation is to be rendered by the

---

[7] H. R. Garvin, "Gertrude Stein: A Study of Her Theory and Practice," unpublished doctoral dissertation (Michigan, 1950), p. 124.

presentation of the situation itself and not to be imposed on the situation through the impact of the style.

Whereas Gertrude Stein uses her narrator to *approximate* the rhythm of Negro speech, she also uses the dialogue of her characters in much the same way. It must be obvious that Miss Stein is not interested in reproducing dialogue with the exactness of a tape recorder. The penchant for giving literal, almost phonetic transcriptions of dialect is something that Gertrude Stein decidedly does not share with the realists. Since the entire story is an attempt at an approximation of reality rather than a reproduction of it, Gertrude Stein feels the freedom is hers to control the dialogue so that it aids in the sense of the continuous present she is attempting to give in her manipulation of the time continuum. As an abstractionist, Miss Stein accepts all the elements of the work of fiction as plastic entities subject to her needs.

One can choose almost any long passage of dialogue at random from "Melanctha" to see that it is not at all Miss Stein's concern to reproduce with verbal exactitude the inflections in the speech of Jeff and Melanctha.

> "I know Miss Melanctha" he began, "It ain't very easy for you to understand what I was meaning by what I was just saying to you, and perhaps some of the good people I like so wouldn't think very much, any more than you do, Miss Melanctha, about the ways I have to be good. But that's no matter Miss Melanctha. What I mean Miss Melanctha by what I was just saying to you is, that I don't, no, never, believe in doing things just to get excited. You see Miss Melanctha I mean the way so many of the colored people do it." (121)

This particular passage goes on for another full, uninterrupted page. First of all, dialogue that goes on so long at such a relaxed pace without an interruption by one of the partners violates one of the conventions of realistic literary dialogue as well as ordinary conversation. If this were the only instance of a protracted speech in "Melanctha," we could legitimately call it an exception, but it is only one of many such speeches. Secondly, Jeff adopts one of the conventions of the narrative in the use of the present participle in his opening sentence. Thirdly, the speeches here and elsewhere in "Melanctha" take on a syntactic and ideational complexity on their own level that is the equal of the most analytic Henry James speech. This complexity is surely not justified "realistically" in the context of the primitive level of behavior we see exhibited by the characters of the story.

What then is Gertrude Stein trying to do here? It seems to this reader, at any rate, that the dialogue of a Gertrude Stein story attempts to suggest the tone or syntax of Negro speech while preserving the analytic point of view she takes toward her characters. Gertrude Stein wants us to see the primitive consciousness of her characters' minds at work, while at the same time suggesting the ethnic qualities of their speech patterns. In order to do this, Miss Stein feels she must abandon the contemporary conventions of realistic dialogue and establish conventions of her own.

Even the letters that Jeff and Melanctha exchange are more approximations of the mentalities of the writers than they are "real" letters. No literate individual (which Jeff demonstrably is), no matter how he spoke the English language, would write a serious letter to his lover that began like this:

Dear Melanctha, I certainly do know you ain't been any way sick this last week when you never met me right the way you promised, and never sent me any word to say why you acted a way you certainly never could think was the right way you should do it to me. (191)

In many ways the above is almost a parody of lower-class, illiterate Negro speech. Granted that being a physician does not require Jeff Campbell to speak like a member of the Modern Language Association; but if such a passage were to emanate from the mouth of a doctor even in a Dreiser novel it would be ludicrous. If we are able to accept this in "Melanctha," however, if we are able here to "suspend our disbelief," it is almost certainly due to the fact that Gertrude Stein has forced us to accept her conventions as outlined above, and we subject a passage such as this to the same kind of scrutiny we would extend to a passage of dialogue spoken by the same character.

If her characters show an analytic turn of mind in their speeches and thoughts, they are also quite ruminative. Existing on a primitive ideational level, they repeat themselves constantly as they torturously analyze the problems that obsess them. But whereas this renders the movement of the novel almost static, there is nonetheless a rationale for this seemingly annoying trait. For instance, Jeff's repetitive ruminations are simply the reflection of a mind that is slow-moving, anxious, and indecisive. Jeff is constantly trying to justify his own actions and rationalize his motives. He constantly regurgitates the same problems to discuss them over and over again either with Melanctha or in his own mind. But his mind is not incisive enough to see to the heart of his problem, and so he is forced into an endless cycle of repetition. This abstract (in the sense of our definition of the term) repetitiveness is then a reflection of the very nature of the characters as Gertrude Stein establishes them.

The "talky" quality of so much of "Melanctha" is another reflection of Gertrude Stein's abstract concerns. Events in "Melanctha" have almost no dramatic importance whatsoever. Miss Stein emphasizes the actual event just as little as she emphasizes the actual physical object. The importance of the event lies not in its place in the narrative chain, but in its effect on the life and especially the consciousness of the characters. Whatever happens to Jeff and Melanctha they discuss or mull over endlessly. The event itself assumes its significance only through what we learn about it through the expression of either of the characters or through the narrator's speaking in the accents of the characters. Since almost everything in the story is an outgrowth of the consciousness of Jeff or Melanctha, the language is infused with an obvious talkiness. And yet, it is only through this talkiness that we can follow the actual train of the narrative. We see narrative development only in the subtle changes and gradations in the interpersonal relationships of the book that show themselves in the characters' discussions of their own lives. Once again we see that language, structure, and content work inextricably together in "Melanctha."

One of the most discussed characteristics of Gertrude Stein's abstract style is her use of repetition. I have pointed out characteristics of repetition previously in our discussion of "The Good Anna" and "The Gentle Lena." We have seen in the paragraph just previous to this one the repetitious quality of the conversations and thoughts of Jeff and Melanctha. Miss Stein seems to view life as a succession of moments, each one of which repeats all the characteristics of the previous one with a very slight addition of some sort. All her writings exemplify this notion to some degree, structuring themselves by a long series of accretions of miniscule change. Repetition becomes basic to Miss Stein's aesthetic in *Three Lives,* and to those characteristics of repetition we have considered in the two shorter tales of *Three Lives* we shall add a few in "Melanctha."

First of all, Miss Stein develops certain *motifs* either of single words or phrases which she repeats at significant intervals in her story. One is "the wide abandoned laughter that makes the warm broad glow of negro sunshine." Gertrude Stein uses this phrase to describe the various Negroes that she introduces into the narrative. Where the particular character stands with regard to this characteristic usually defines the nature of his personality.

Rose [Johnson] laughed when she was happy but she had not the wide, abandoned laughter that makes the warm broad glow of negro sunshine. (86)

In the days when he [Melanctha's father] had been most young and free and open, he had never had the wide abandoned laughter that gives the broad glow to negro sunshine. (92)

He [Jeff Campbell] sang when he was happy and he laughed, and his was the free abandoned laughter that gives the warm broad glow to negro sunshine. (111)

There are also certain variations on the same phrase:

He [Jeff Campbell] always had a warm broad glow, like southern sunshine. (137)

These were pleasant days then, in the hot southern negro sunshine . . . (209)

"Yes, Melanctha, darling," murmured Jeff, and he was very happy in it, and so the two of them now in the warm air of the sultry, southern, negro sunshine, lay there for a long time just resting. (161)

Certain key words are used again and again in the text as *leitmotifs* of a sort. For instance, Melanctha's journey through life in search of experience is in *Three Lives* called "wandering" in search of "wisdom." These terms assume a special meaning in Miss Stein's usage. The kind of "wisdom" Melanctha desires most particularly is sexual. This variety of knowledge is obtainable only through "wandering" from one sexual experience to another. Early in the story Melanctha is not prepared to do the proper wandering requisite for wisdom. She receives her first training from Jane Harden, who is well versed in these areas. Although there are homosexual implications in the relationship of Jane Harden and Melanctha, especially in the way Jane turns on Melanctha later on, this kind of "wandering" is simply another way of attaining the nebulous "wisdom."

Once the meanings of these terms are established, Miss Stein is then able to vary the usage. In much the same way as with the quotation previously considered, these two terms are used as descriptive evaluations against which to measure the various characters we meet in the book.

"Mis" Herbert had always been a little wandering and mysterious and uncertain in her ways. (90)

Jem Richards always had known what it was to have real wisdom. (217)

And so Melanctha wandered on the edge of wisdom. (101)

To heighten the special meaning of these *motif*-words Miss Stein occasionally uses the terms with their conventional meanings. After one of their reconciliations Jeff and Melanctha pack food and go out to walk in the country. Their "wandering" on this day is quite innocent.

They were very happy all that day in their wandering. They had taken things along to eat together. They sat in the bright fields and they were happy, they wandered in the woods and they were happy. Jeff always loved in this way to wander. (149)

In the usage which Miss Stein creates for these words in "Melanctha," we can see for the first time evidence of a later major characteristic of her writing: the creation of new meanings for old words.

Aside from the use of repetition as *leitmotif,* we see in "Melanctha" isolated instances of repetition for sheer emphasis, allied with a spirit of play. On page 143, the last long paragraph on the page shows every sentence beginning with either the words "Jane Harden" or the word "Jane." On page 165, to mention another instance, the words "always" or "always now" appear in nearly every sentence. It would be impossible to justify this merely as repetition for the purposes of emphasis. This kind of emphasis has all the subtlety of a pounding hammer. It is Miss Stein's spirit of play that is at work here, an element to which she gives ever freer rein throughout her career. We would do well to come to terms with this clownish side of Gertrude Stein as early as possible.

An element of Gertrude Stein's use of "wander" and "wisdom" leads to a further facet of her abstract style, the use of euphemisms. Aside from her lack of specificity in descriptive fact and setting, Miss Stein shows a decided reticence toward subjects such as sexual matters that she seems to find distasteful. Rather than more pointed terminology for sexual behavior and object she uses such general terms as "wander" and "wisdom." When Jeff begins to feel a growing attraction for Melanctha, Gertrude Stein describes it in the following fashion:

> When anything amused him in them [the newspapers] he read it out to Melanctha. Melanctha was now pretty silent, with him. Dr. Campbell began to feel a little, about how she responded to him. Dr. Campbell began to see a little that perhaps Melanctha had a good mind. Dr. Campbell was not sure yet that she had a good mind, but he began to think a little that perhaps she might have one. (116)

It is surely not Melanctha's mind that is attracting Jeff Campbell, whatever else it may be. Indeed, it is almost humorous how Gertrude Stein avoids being explicit about sexual matters. Richard Bridgman has pointed out how Gertrude Stein describes Melanctha's early "wanderings" in almost symbolic terms, placing them in the setting of a railroad yard amid "the full rush of the pounding train, that bursts out from the tunnel where it lost itself," (98) among train men who ask her, " 'Hullo sis, do you want to sit on my engine?' " When dared to climb onto a high place by one of the workmen, she fell and broke her arm, an act to which "it is difficult not to assign some hymeneal meaning."[8] It is easy to become impatient with Gertrude Stein for this kind of ambiguity

8 Richard Bridgman, "Melanctha," *Am. Lit.,* XXXIII (Nov. 1961), 354.

and obfuscation, but let us remember first that Henry
James takes us completely through *The Wings of the
Dove* without telling us the nature of Milly Theale's ill-
ness and through *The Ambassadors* without telling what
it is that the Newsomes manufacture.

One other point that must be explored before we leave
"Melanctha" is Gertrude Stein's continuing and strength-
ening notions of personality. The concern with the racial
type is still very much present.

> Rose Johnson was careless and was lazy, but she had been
> brought up by white folks and she needed decent comfort. Her
> white training had only made for habits, not for nature. Rose
> had the simple, promiscuous unmorality of the black people.
> (86)

The social class type:

> Rose now *in the easy fashion of the poor* lived with one
> woman in her house, and then for no reason went and lived
> with some other woman in her house. (88, italics mine)

In these she goes no farther than with similar passages in
"The Good Anna" or "The Gentle Lena." In her discussion of personality types, however, she does at one point
set off in a new direction. On page 186 there are two
paragraphs that carry on at some length about "tender
hearted natures" and "passionate natures," prefiguring
the much longer discussion of various types of human
personality that Gertrude Stein undertakes in *The Making
of Americans*. The first paragraph begins:

> In tender hearted natures, those that mostly never feel strong
> passion, suffering often comes to make them harder. (186)

The paragraph continues for another eleven lines in the
same vein, containing some of the thoughts of the nar-

rator and some of Jeff Campbell. The second paragraph
begins:

> Passionate natures who have always made themselves, to
> suffer, that is all the kind of people who have emotions that
> come to them as sharp as a sensation, they always get more
> tender-hearted when they suffer, and it always does them good
> to suffer.

Before it is over, this paragraph goes on to include a
small discussion of "comfortable natures." Gertrude
Stein's next book will be focused entirely on personality
types.

What effect does this concern have on her treatment
of the characters in "Melanctha?" Let us look for our
evidence in the main character herself. As we have discussed at length earlier, Gertrude Stein is a psychological determinist. Those psychological characteristics that
make up a personality, those traits that a character
shares with a certain "type," determine the actions and
the entire behavior patterns connected with the individual in question. One of the first determinants of personality for Gertrude Stein is heredity. We have already discussed heredity in connection with Melanctha in our
opening remarks about the tale. Gertrude Stein sets forth
this problem explicitly early in the story:

> Melanctha was pale yellow and mysterious and a little pleasant
> like her mother, but the real power in Melanctha's nature came
> through her robust and unpleasant and very unendurable black
> father. (90)

> She [Melanctha] had not been raised like Rose by white
> folks but then she had been half made with real white blood.
> (86)

The mixed racial heritage and the inherited personality traits of her parents seem to Gertrude Stein to be the major factors determining the composition of the personality known as Melanctha. Just where Melanctha would fit into the type-structure Miss Stein erects in *The Making of Americans* we will not venture to guess. What she does have in common with the rest of Gertrude Stein's fictional characters is the fixed, repetitive nature of the actions that grow inevitably out of her personality. Melanctha is one whose contours cannot be seen out of the context of her relationships with other characters, and her actions follow the same pattern throughout the story. Melanctha can find no middle ground with another person. She is either dominant or dominated. Her relationships always begin with her being submissive to the other partner. This is the pattern she establishes with Jane Harden and Jeff Campbell. After she has gotten what she wants with each, however, she suddenly takes the upper hand and with almost cruel disdain excises the other person from her life. With Jem Richards she begins the same way, but as the relationship progresses we become aware that Melanctha has more than met her match. And yet, this seems to be what she has wanted all along, perhaps in a Freudian way through the influence of her cruelly dominant father. Gertrude Stein gives the clue to this quite early:

> He was a reckless man was Jem Richards. He knew how to win out, and always all her life, Melanctha Herbert loved successful power. (217)

Melanctha always "loved successful power," but it is her particular cross that those who wield the successful power will always do her in, just as she left Jeff and Jane Harden when she was finished with them. As soon as things get too hot in Bridgepoint for Jem Richards, he leaves town and Melanctha. As soon as Rose Johnson feels Melanctha threatening her husband, she tells her to go away. Once again Melanctha is turned away by someone who is dominant over her. After this final rejection Melanctha's life begins to trail off to its end.

A very strong impression that one gets from a reading of "Melanctha" is that there has been no equivocation possible of the pattern of her life. Melanctha could go through a thousand reincarnations, and in not one would her life be very different. For a while she could perhaps dominate the weak, but ultimately she would be beaten down by someone stronger than she. And since she is one to whom living means experiencing at its highest pitch, her defeats would ultimately mean her destruction. There is something monolithic and abstract about such a static conception of personality. Though critics have been concerned with the similarities between "Melanctha" and *Things as They Are*,[9] it seems to me that the most profound similarity between the two tales lies in the conception of the personality of the central figure in each of the stories. Both Adele and Melanctha are "slow-moving" people who are dependent on others in relationships. No matter how many relationships they enter into or how many times they try to make the present one

---

[9] Bridgman, *op. cit.,* and Sutherland, *op. cit.* Leo Stein made the claim in *Journey into the Self* that "Melanctha" was simply a reworking of the materials of *Things as They Are*. In its most literal sense, this statement is a gross oversimplification. However, there are a number of similarities between the two works, some of which are discussed above. The best documentation of these similarities occurs in the opening pages of Richard Bridgman's article on "Melanctha."

succeed, they are always doomed to the same outcome. They are victimized by stronger characters. Their personalities are fixed.

There are other minor similarities between the two early books. Jeff accuses Melanctha: "You certainly ain't got no right to be always holding your pain out to me." (172) This is reminiscent of a similar accusation that Adele makes of Helen in *Things as They Are.*[10] Melanctha as a child suffers stoically with a broken arm that her father refuses to have tended by a doctor. The almost exact situation is described in the earlier book in connection with Helen. Throughout "Melanctha," crucial situations between Jeff and Melanctha are always saved at the last minute by Jeff's taking her emotionally into his arms. The same pattern occurs repeatedly in *Things as They Are.*

Other similarities could be listed. However, from our point of view the two books are more interesting for their differences than merely for what they have in common, most of which we have already discussed. Perhaps the main difference still to be considered is that the focus in "Melanctha" is reduced from the relationship of three characters to that of two. For almost one hundred pages in the center of the story Gertrude Stein allows nothing to intrude on Jeff and Melanctha. Other backgrounds and characters sink almost into nonexistence. We shall see the focus reduced even further in the works that follow. *The Making of Americans* will focus on the individual character, although in the general con-

[10] " 'You have no right to constantly use your pain as a weapon!' Adele flashed out angrily." *Things as They Are* (Pawlet, Vt., 1950), p. 60.

text of the other characters. The "portraits" will focus almost purely on the one character, with only the hint of an observer. *Tender Buttons* will focus on simple physical objects.

Three Lives, especially "Melanctha," is then a genuine step into the abstract style. While it does not go as far as later works toward the abolition of all narrative movement and verisimilitude, it establishes all the strains that Gertrude Stein is to develop in her first major style, as represented by *The Making of Americans,* and in the later styles of her "portraits" and *Tender Buttons.*

4

The Making of Americans

BY THE TIME SHE HAD FINISHED *Three Lives,* GERTRUDE Stein was already looking ahead to the major work she was to write next. The many unpublished charts and notebooks that lie in the Yale Collection of American Literature are testimony to the intense amount of preparation Miss Stein did before sitting down to begin *The Making of Americans.* When she finally began the writing she worked at the book on and off for the next five years. Donald Gallup, Miss Stein's literary executor, has carefully dated the composition of the book.

Begun at Fiesole in the summer of 1906, shortly after the completion of the stories later published as *Three Lives,* it seems to have been worked at more or less continuously until the end of 1908. Then other works, notably "A Long Gay Book," "Two," "Many Many Women" and a great number of the portraits, were begun and carried along while *The Mak-*

ing of Americans was still in progress, and the final section of the novel was not completed until October 1911.[1]

After working on the book for two years Miss Stein's restless mind went out in search of a new style in new works. She tells us about this throughout *The Making of Americans,* and she demonstrates some of her new techniques late in the book.

Most readers know *The Making of Americans* only in the abridged version published by Harcourt, Brace in 1934 to coincide with Gertrude Stein's triumphant return to the United States. This version reprints the sections of the original version that Bernard Faÿ chose for his French translation of the book, and received the approval of the author. Indeed, Miss Stein quotes from this edition in her lecture on "The Gradual Making of The Making of Americans [*sic*]."[2] Nowhere in this book do the publishers tell the reader that he is reading an abridgment. As a result, many readers do not know that the original version of *The Making of Americans* was published in 1925[3] and ran to 925 closely printed pages, as against 416 of the more liberally spaced abridgment. Although the original version has assumed today the status of a very rare book, I shall be referring to *it* rather than the merely scarce abridged version, since the former is Miss Stein's own conception of what the book should be.

The full-length *Making of Americans* is one of the major "unread" modern books. Its overwhelming length and the difficulties posed by its style have presented ob-

[1] "The Making of *The Making of Americans,*" *New Colophon,* III (1950), 54.
[2] *Lectures in America* (Boston, 1957), pp. 135-161.
[3] Contact Editions.

stacles that have proved insurmountable to most critics. Edmund Wilson, who gave Gertrude Stein the critical status of a modern classic in *Axel's Castle,* admits in the same book that "I confess that I have not read this book all through, and I do not know whether it is possible to do so."[4] Ben Reid is even more assertive:

> The complete *Making of Americans* is, I am convinced, unreadable for a normal mind. I have read every word of the shortened version (I think I have—it's hard to be sure), but I am not proud of the accomplishment, and I doubt that a score of people could be found who have done even that.[5]

It is obvious that we have entered the realm of those of Gertrude Stein's works that have posed enigmas to almost all of her readers. Although Donald Sutherland has said that "the work itself, the sequence of statements and ideas, makes the stream of thought perfectly objective and available to anyone who can read English,"[6] it is obvious to any reader of *The Making of Americans* that its difficulties go well beyond the fact that all the sentences and paragraphs make individual sense and that there is a certain connection between paragraphs and the larger units of the book. *The Making of Americans* takes a number of bold strides into the kingdom of the abstract, and any reader who brings with him only the equipment needed to approach a novel of traditional realism will react in much the same way as Mr. Wilson or Mr. Reid.

The Making of Americans was first published almost

---

[4] New York, 1931, p. 239.

[5] *Art by Subtraction: A Dissenting Opinion of Gertrude Stein* (Norman, Okla., 1958), p. 18.

[6] *Gertrude Stein: A Biography of Her Work* (New Haven, 1951), p. 55.

twenty years after it was begun. Alice B. Toklas tells us
how Gertrude Stein had no luck at all finding a pub-
lisher, and how the original manuscript languished for
many years in their apartment, unread except by the
closest devotees of her circle.[7] Finally, in 1923, Ernest
Hemingway offered to help get the book published in
installments in Ford Madox Ford's *Transatlantic Review*.
At this point Miss Stein picked up the manuscript once
again and with the help of Miss Toklas and Hemingway
began to get it ready for publication. Complications surrounding the printing of installments in Ford's magazine
led eventually to a falling out with Ford, but the public
notice accorded the work brought about the publication
of the complete book by Robert McAlmon's Contact
Press in 1925, and to the Boni and Liveright edition of
the following year.

In addition to a quite substantial body of notes, outlines and charts, and a complete typescript, there are
two complete autograph manuscript versions of *The
Making of Americans* in the Yale Collection of American
Literature.[8] There is also a small ledger with a draft of
what Gertrude Stein originally numbered the first five
chapters that is previous to either of the complete versions. Miss Stein copied her own work endlessly and
often made extensive revisions, interpolations, and ex-
cisions. Faced with material of this sort, one of the problems of this study becomes the determination of which

[7] Gertrude Stein, *The Autobiography of Alice B. Toklas* (New
York, 1933), p. 215.
[8] I must here express my thanks to Mr. Donald Gallup, curator of
the Yale Collection of American Literature, for making my examination of Gertrude Stein's letters and manuscripts both free from difficulty and profitable.

stylistic revisions were made when Gertrude Stein prepared the text for publication in the 1920's. Since the manuscript of *The Making of Americans*, not including the typescript, fills five boxes, a line-by-line comparison of manuscript and published text is not practicable for this study. (The final autograph manuscript fills twenty-seven large composition-size notebooks on both sides of the page.) However, a careful study of a number of random selections from *The Making of Americans* shows that even in her later revisions Gertrude Stein remained essentially faithful to the spirit of her earlier abstract style. The revisions consist mainly of changing certain words that Miss Stein presumably found ungraceful and of exchanging certain phrases for others that were perhaps more satisfactory to her ear; but in no significant way do they tamper with the spirit of the early style.

There is one change in the later manuscript that is worth noting as a minor revision of some significance. Throughout the entire earlier manuscript version Gertrude Stein kept one autobiographical element constantly at work. She referred to the Hersland family as "german." This descriptive adjective we find lined through in all the later manuscript versions and omitted altogether in the published book. In the manuscript, for instance, there appears the sentence, "This [*sic*] german men and women, our grandfathers and grandmothers, with their children born and unborn with them . . ." In the book this appears as "These certain men and women . . ."[9] This constant excision throughout the book reduces Gertrude Stein's autobiographical role for one

[9] Gertrude Stein, *The Making of Americans* (Paris, 1925), p. 3. Page numbers in text refer to this edition.

thing, but more important, it renders the descriptions of the Herslands less specific, and thus they become even more solidly portrayed general types.[10]

A more profitable contrast can be made between the earliest extant version of *The Making of Americans* and the drafts that follow. Many of the passages that appear in this early manuscript version disappear altogether later on. The reason for this is fairly clear. Most of the passages that disappear are the equal of many of the most awkward passages of *Things as They Are*. The kind of apprentice work that these excised passages seem to be leads one to believe that this opening was written a long time previous to the rest of the book. Perhaps it antedates *Three Lives,* although there seems to be no way to prove this.[11] The opening passage of the book begins:

> Once an angry man dragged his father along the ground through his own orchard. "Stop!" cried the groaning old man at last, "Stop! I did not drag my father beyond this tree."

[10] It has been suggested by Drs. Roland Gibson and Herbert Howarth that Gertrude Stein excised the word "german" because of the anti-German climate in Europe following the World War.

[11] One of the difficulties in dealing with Gertrude Stein's manuscript notebooks is that they may contain excerpts from a number of works begun at different times. And since she was in the habit of beginning occasionally toward the end of the notebook, we cannot merely suppose that the portions of the manuscript were written in the order that they appear. An example should make my point. There is a notebook among the notes to *The Making of Americans* that begins quite expectedly with a passage that in slightly revised form appears later in the published version of the book. It concerns the ancestry and general qualities of men and women from *The Making of Americans*. Then there appear five or six pages of an unpublished fable about a man who had three sons and did not know which was the true one. Following that is a section from *The Making of Americans* on "thinking ourselves always to be young men and women." Then there is a short fragment from *The Making of Americans*

This did not appear at all in the earliest draft, but makes its first appearance in the second draft as follows:

> There is an old story that tells of a man who, merciless in his anger, dragged his father along the ground through his own orchard.
> "John stop," cried the groaning old man . . .

It is instructive to consider the changes made here by Miss Stein for the final version. One could feel that the original passage was more abstract (by our definition) because its anecdotal tone prevents the establishment of a feeling of verisimilitude, whereas the way the lines now stand they plunge us directly into the narrative. There are a number of reasons, however, why this is not so. First of all, the general nature of the narrative gives it an almost fable-like quality. Time is designated merely as "once." The characters are identified no more closely

---

about "one of these 4 german [sic] women." After this is a section about the young Dehnings. Then facing the section on the Dehnings, and running concurrently for three or four pages, we see a passage from "Melanctha" about Melanctha and Rose Johnson that appears with revisions late in the published version of that story. These fragments vary between pen and pencil, between sloppy and careful penmanship. (When Miss Stein uses careful penmanship it almost certainly means that she is making a copy of an earlier draft.) There is no very good way of determining when any of them were written, except to suppose that it was no later than 1906, the *terminus ad quem* of *Three Lives*. Since "Melanctha" was the last written of *Three Lives,* it is altogether possible that it was written concurrently with the early notes to *The Making of Americans*. Or if Miss Stein followed her common practice of beginning a notebook toward the end, perhaps she merely picked a scarcely used notebook from *Three Lives* and began to use it for the notes for her next work. But then how do we explain the appearance of the unpublished fable? When was it written, and what work was it to be a part of, if any? These questions are perhaps unanswerable. At any rate, the problems of establishing an absolute order for the earliest of the Stein canon should be clear.

than "an angry man" and "his father." The setting is merely "the ground" in the father's "own orchard." Since we do not even know who the father is, the information hardly places us in a specific locale. In fact, almost nothing is localized. We are in a timeless world anywhere. Even the name "John" that appeared in the earlier draft has been excised by Gertrude Stein. The central fictional character of this piece of narrative is nameless. The passage as it now stands is from this point of view still quite abstract.

However, another even more important reason for its abstractionist superiority over its earlier version is seen in its juxtaposition with the general statement that follows, which begins: "It is hard living down the tempers we are born with." Each passage is made more meaningful by the juxtaposition's forcing us to make a difficult connection between the two paragraphs. Had the opening paragraph been left as a piece of semi-abstract narrative the contrast between the two passages would not have been nearly as striking.

Two major sources of abstractionism in *The Making of Americans* are the increased use of repetition in sentence structure and the further extension of the kind of syntactic discontinuity we found in *Three Lives*. Stylistic concerns for Gertrude Stein now begin to override plot, movement, setting, and character development. *The Making of Americans* is almost completely a novel of description, 925 pages of pure "telling." Gertrude Stein is obviously the narrator from the very first word, and she constantly places her own ideas before the reader. There is no attempt to make the narrative move, to give the illusion of life passing before your eyes. What Gertrude

Stein attempts to do in this mammoth chronicle is give a
sense of the slow, evergoing passage of time from moment to moment and from generation to generation, and
her various uses of repetition are her major means to this
end. We see the continuous cycle of time moving in endless repetitions as the continuous present unfolds itself. If
there is movement, it is contained not in the intercourse
between human beings, but within each present moment
and its movement to its successor.

In addition to the use of repetition, Gertrude Stein
employs another set of devices to give her sentences the
variety that lends her style much of whatever else it may
have of individuality and distinction. What Miss Stein
sets up for us in the style of this book is the traditional
straightforward English syntax of sentence-verb-ob-
ject and its variations. Since we come to all writings in
English with this expectancy, Miss Stein merely reinforces
our expectations with her opening sentences. This is exactly what almost all the books within the reading experience of all of us do. Of course, what gives all writing
whatever we call its unique style arises from the variations that the individual author imposes on the standard
patterns of the language. Writing that lacks such variations as figurative language, imagery, metaphor, and all
the many well-known figures would have the stylistic
interest of a telephone book, or, charitably, of a very dull
newspaper. Gertrude Stein does not use to a great extent
many of the standard figures that authors have used to
vary their prose patterns. Aside from repetition, she uses
disorienting devices to wrench her sentence structure
from the standard syntax. Some of these devices include:
the completion of phrases normally left "understood" by

most speakers and writers of English; the use of certain words in functions normally foreign to words of their particular morphology; the dislocation of standard word order in places that the traditional user of the English language would normally avoid. It is through variations such as these, however, that the qualities of Gertrude Stein's writing that we have dubbed abstractionism increasingly manifest themselves. In many of her later writings these qualities of style are almost the only thing that Gertrude Stein has left us to talk about.

Despite its great length, *The Making of Americans* is centrally concerned with only a handful of characters from the Hersland family, Julia Dehning who marries Alfred Hersland, and a few seamstresses, governesses, and friends who wander in and out of the lives of the main figures in the book. John Malcolm Brinnin has made the following mathematical calculations:

Two hundred and eighty-eight pages are devoted to heredity and "the old people in the new world." One hundred and ninety-eight pages are devoted to Martha Hersland who is of "the new people made out of the old" . . . Two hundred and forty-four pages are given to Alfred Hersland and Julia Dehning . . . One hundred and eighty-four pages are devoted to David Hersland . . .[12]

In each of these sections we discover the life story of one of the various central characters, although we certainly do not follow them from the cradle to the grave in that order. We follow the older generation from Europe to the United States. We see them settle in Bridgepoint and then in Gossols, without our knowing where either

[12] *The Third Rose: Gertrude Stein and Her World* (Boston, 1959), p. 95.

of these places is. We see the children develop, marry, have a few friends, governesses, and seamstresses, and die. The actual events of the book could probably be counted on fingers and toes, and most of them are not events that we witness, but that we are told about. It is almost impossible to retell the plot coherently because there is genuinely no such thing. What Gertrude Stein presents us is simply a series of character studies, and the emphasis is decidedly on *character*. Events come into focus not when they supposedly happened but when they suddenly become relevant to illustrate a point that the author wishes to make. Gertrude Stein has succeeded almost completely in getting away from the notion of "story." This in itself is a very large step away from "Melanctha" in the direction of total abstractionism.

If there is no time sequence, almost no events, and no story, then *The Making of Americans* is recognizable as a novel only in the loosest contemporary definition of the term. What then is it? Rather than get ourselves mired in the sticky mud of rigid definition, let us examine what Gertrude Stein herself had to say about it. The subtitle of the book is "The History of a Family's Progress." Is *The Making of Americans* a history? (*Three Lives* was originally titled *Three Histories*.) If history is the chronological reporting of events in time, then we must give only the most guarded yes as answer to the question. Gertrude Stein does not care about the ordering of events in time. One of the demands she makes on the reader in this book is that he reorder the history for himself if he wants to follow a time continuum. However, there is enough else in Gertrude Stein's method that reminds us of historical writing to allow us to go on with the analogy. In a history one tells what happened, or at least attempts to do so. Most of the time one does not try to render or reproduce the events of the past just as they supposedly occurred to create the illusion of verisimilitude. One tells what the events were and perhaps analyzes the possible reasons for their occurrence, or presents the possible causes of the event and then presents the event as growing out of the causes. In many respects, these are at least a partial explanation for Gertrude Stein's literary method in *The Making of Americans*. She tells and she analyzes, or she does the reverse. She is not interested in presenting a realistic reproduction of the event, only its implications. She is perhaps what one could call an interpretive historian, with the emphasis on *interpretive*. In fact, the emphasis is so much on the interpretive that her documentation is weak. I am, however, not attempting to pass judgment on Miss Stein as an historian, but merely to characterize her as such. Most of the time one must accept what she says in her explanations of various characters. She does not like to waste time exemplifying her statements by having her fictional people perform in various situations.

That Gertrude Stein looked on herself as a kind of historian is evident from statements that she makes during the course of the book:

Sometime there is a history of each one. There must be such a history of each one for the repeating in them makes a history of them. The repeating of the kinds of them makes a history of the kinds of them, the repeating of the different parts and ways of being makes a history in many ways of every one. This is now a history of some. This will be sometime a history of many kinds of them. Any one who looks at each one will see coming out from them the bottom nature of them and the mixing of other nature or natures with the bottom nature of them. (190-91)

We must, however, look on Gertrude Stein as a historian of the individual consciousness rather than as one of the more conventional types of historians. Gertrude Stein treats her characters more as potentially historical figures than as fictional ones: "Sometime there will be a complete history of Madeleine Wyman's married living, it will be very interesting." (265) It would seem safe to say that Gertrude Stein's attitude and method place *The Making of Americans* in a genre somewhere between the loosely defined modern novel and the narrowly defined history of personal consciousness. Whatever name one gives it, however, it seems obvious that *The Making of Americans* makes a genuine break away from the tradition of the novel as Gertrude Stein found it.

The structure of *The Making of Americans* is in many ways a logical extension of the method Gertrude Stein was exploring in *Three Lives*. For one thing, it lacks even more the specific description of the realistic novel. There is no sense of time setting, for all its similarity to history. The fable-like tone noted in the opening lines of the novel extends to the sense of time in the book as a whole. Gertrude Stein is at great pains to let us know that this family could be any family anywhere in America at any time, and the same characteristics would be true of its individual members. And so, she does not bother to give any indication as to when the events of the novel take place or when the characters lived.

The same thing is true of the attention that Gertrude Stein lavishes on the physical setting. She is careful to tell us what class of people live in particular sections of the town, but we have next to no idea what the houses look like and only an inkling of where the towns are located. (Oakland and Baltimore are presumably the real-life counterparts of Gossols and Bridgepoint, but of this we cannot be absolutely certain.) Of course, Bridge-point is the same town that served as the setting for *Three Lives,* only we have moved up many notches in the social scale in the characters that demand our attention. The one sense of description that continues almost intact from Miss Stein's previous works is the sense of social milieu. Although she avoids many specific descriptions here, Gertrude Stein gives us a very strong sense of the social circles in which her characters live.

Another logical extension of the methodology of *Three Lives* is the fracturing of time that Gertrude Stein carries to far greater lengths than in "Melanctha." In the former book, Miss Stein began the narrative with the action in the present, moved back to the past, and then continued through the past back into the present time once again. We were required to keep in our minds the information we got in the beginning of the story until the end when the events took place all over again. However, what was required there was nothing when compared to the extent to which Miss Stein breaks up the time sequence in *The Making of Americans.* If we are required to wait 125 pages for the return of Rose Johnson and the birth of her baby in the earlier book, Miss Stein now asks us to wait 600 pages for some events to recur and some characters to reappear. In the earliest part of the book we witness the wedding preparations and marriage of Julia Dehning and Alfred Hersland. After this the subject is dropped until page 647, when we are suddenly presented once again with the event, which we are of course expected to remember.

But there is something that further complicates this kind of difficulty. In "Melanctha" the time sequence which Gertrude Stein proceeds to violate is quite obvious; it is defined by the length of Melanctha's life. But *The Making of Americans* deals with generations of individuals whose lives cross so much in a temporally and spatially undefined universe that we find it almost impossible to reconstruct any line of continuity.

As in "Melanctha," we have here the same presentness of time, even with events that are supposedly occurring in the distant past. The moment in which the events happen is always a present moment. Miss Stein wreaks such havoc with the traditional continuum of time that the only time we can see with any surety is the present moment in which a particular passage was created—or perhaps is being read. Of course, if all time is continually present, then all time can never be either past or future. That is perhaps why in Gertrude Stein there is ultimately no looking backward or forward in time. There is only the now.

An even further violation of time is brought about by one of Gertrude Stein's major devices for violating the continuity of the structure of the story line. I refer now to her use of the generalized digression. We have noticed the digression as an element that appeared almost gratuitously tacked on to the story in *Things as They Are*. In *Three Lives* we found that the digression by the narrator usually served to describe the particular type, be it social, psychological, or racial, that the narrator felt himself called upon to define. However, what we have nominally been recognizing as a disgression becomes in *The Making of Americans* a most integral part of the narrative method. In this book Miss Stein is so concerned with her characters as examples of various psychological types that she is as much or more concerned with the description of the type as with the description of the person. One of her standard methods for presenting her characters is to introduce them and tell about a few of their characteristics in a single rounded paragraph. In the following paragraph she leaves the specific world of her character and begins to list in her peculiar repetitive style the characteristics of the type which by its juxtaposition we take to be related to the character of the preceding paragraph. This manner of presenting the material Gertrude Stein generally follows throughout the course of her book, alternating her paragraphs between those of description and those of generalized digression.

This is now a history of Martha Hersland. This is now a history of Martha and of everyone who came to be of her living.

There will then be soon much description of every way one can think of men and women, in their beginning, in their middle living, and their ending.

Every one then is an individual being. Every one then is like many others always living, there are many ways of thinking of every one, this is now a description of all of them. There must then be a whole history of each one of them. There must then now be a description of all repeating. Now I will tell all the meaning to me in repeating, the loving there is in me for repeating. (290)

The character is presented in the opening sentence, and we are told that this will be her history. Then Miss

Stein digresses immediately to a consideration of the meaning of the individual and then to how the individual expresses himself through repetition. In the paragraphs that follow, the generalized disquisitions on the nature of personality types and how they reveal their bottom natures continues, along with a description of Gertrude Stein's own learning processes. Martha Hersland does not reappear for almost twenty pages.

This is now then some description of my learning. Then there will be a beginning again of Martha Hersland and her being and her living. This is now then first a little studying and then later Martha Hersland will begin living. Now then to do this little studying. (308)

She then disappears until page 377, during which time Miss Stein gives her description of the various types of dependent independent, independent dependent, attacking and resisting personalities.

Now then to begin again the history of Martha Hersland and of every one she ever knew in living. Always there will be here writing a description of all the kinds of ways there can be seen to be kinds of men and women. There will be here then written the complete history of every one Martha Hersland ever came to know in her living, the fundamental character of every one, the bottom natures in them, the other natures in them, the mixtures in them, the strength and weakness of everything they have inside them. (377)

Martha Hersland then begins to appear more frequently in her section of the book. Although she is by no means present on every page, she nonetheless rarely disappears for more than a page or two.

It is quite obvious then that the narrative structure of the book is severely stretched. Those who have been trained on prose fiction that presents a story or at least a narrative that can be followed both spatially and temporally (and this really includes all of us) find their attention taxed almost beyond endurance on their first encounter with this book. Never before had a book purporting to be prose narrative fiction played such havoc with the traditional schemes of presentation. Gertrude Stein places us in an abstract world in which the continuity of time almost completely disappears, and all we see are consciousnesses moving perhaps within themselves or in places that have no locality. If, as Gertrude Stein probably would claim, our notions of time and place are conventionalized and have nothing to do with real time or space, we can only answer that we are prisoners of these conventions both in our everyday lives and in the books we have read. To read Gertrude Stein's books from *The Making of Americans* on, we must retrain ourselves in our ways of looking at the world. We can neither condemn nor approve her achievement until we have at least made this attempt.

The narrative method of *The Making of Americans* proceeds directly from the nature of the narrator. In the previous two books, we differentiated between the narrator and Gertrude Stein herself. In each of the books it seemed that Miss Stein was accepting the conventionalized notion that an author keep at least some distance from her book. As a result, in each book she adopted the tone that would seem appropriate to the particular social world she was describing, and she emerged from this tone only occasionally. In this book, too, she adopts a particular stylized form of speaking which she maintains with even more consistency than she did previously.

However, she makes no attempt whatever to remain on the sidelines of her book. She takes part in every bit of the telling from the very first pages. In discussing *The Making of Americans,* then, we shall make no distinction between the narrator and Miss Stein. In fact, the most fruitful way of discussing the narrator's technique is to view it as Gertrude Stein's taking us for a tour through her own creative processes. Perhaps no book since *Tristram Shandy* and until *The Alexandria Quartet* lays bare so much of the way the author went about composing the book. This aspect of Gertrude Stein's narrative technique has been attributed by at least one critic to her experiences in scientific work at Harvard and Johns Hopkins.

Even in *The Making of Americans,* however, Miss Stein, like a scientist, let the reader understand what it was she was doing. A scientist doesn't merely report the conclusions he has reached; he tells also how he reached them. The scientist is at all times a part of the picture. And the novelist, Miss Stein, was a part of the picture of her book all the time.[13]

It will be valuable to keep this astute observation in mind. It is not only Gertrude Stein's constant explanation of her methods that relates her technique to the scientific, but other things such as her use of definition, hypothesis, and demonstration, to which we shall return later in this chapter.

Gertrude Stein's function as narrator constantly has her telling us what she is doing. She tells us her definition of history, as I quoted earlier. She also tells us her method of characterization. In a section of the book con-

[13] George Haines, IV, "Gertrude Stein and Composition," *Sewanee Rev.,* LVII (Summer 1949), 413.

cerned with Alfred Hersland, she has been spending a
great deal of time with her generalized digressions. In
the middle of a paragraph discussing Alfred Hersland's
heredity, she suddenly tells us how she feels about creating him, in terms suggestive of gestation:

> Alfred Hersland then, to be certain of the being in him, was
> of the resisting kind of them in men and women and now then
> I will wait again and soon then I will be full up with him, I
> am now then not completely full up with him. Now I am again
> beginning waiting to be full up completely full up with him. I
> am very considerably full up now with the kind of being in
> him, I will be waiting and then I will be full up with all the
> being in him, that is certain, and so then now a little again
> once more then I am waiting waiting to be filled up full
> completely with him with all the being ever in him. (512-3)

This method may account for the many false stops and
starts we noticed in the sections quoted from the life of
Martha Hersland. Perhaps the digressions cease when
Gertrude Stein is filled up enough with her subject to
begin writing about it.

In other instances Gertrude Stein stops the narrative
or the particular digression on which she is presently
working when she wants to tell us about something she
would like to do or know:

> I want to know sometime all about sentimental feeling. I
> want to know sometime all the different kinds of ways people
> have it in them to be certain of anything. These and virtuous
> feeling in each one, of themselves to themselves having virtue
> inside them, is to me very interesting. Always more and more I
> want to know it of each one what certainty means to them and
> how they come to be certain of anything, what certainty means
> to them and how contradiction does not worry them and how
> it does worry them and how much they have in them of re-

membering and how much they have in them of forgetting, and how different any one is from any other one and what any one and every one means by anything they are saying. All these things are to me very interesting. (480-81)

She tells us of books she wants to write or is perhaps in the process of writing. We must remember that, as Donald Gallup has shown, Miss Stein was working on many other things between 1908 and 1911 when she was finishing *The Making of Americans.*

Sometime then I will give a history of all of them and that will be a long book and when I am finished with this one then I will begin that one. I have already begun that one but now I am still writing on this one and now I am beginning this portion of this one which is the complete history of Alfred Hersland and of every one he ever came to know in living and of many other ones I will be describing now in this beginning. (479)

The book she refers to in this passage is *A Long Gay Book,* which she had obviously already begun.

Miss Stein even makes a series of personal comments about her state of mind during the writing.

I am all unhappy in this writing. I know very much of the meaning of the being in men and women. I know it and feel it and I am always learning more of it and now I am telling it and I am nervous and driving and unhappy in it. Sometimes I will be all happy in it. (348)

In every sense of the idea we are with the author as she creates her book. She conceals nothing from us. As a genuine primitive she does not depend on tricks for her effects but rather keeps everything out in the open where we can see what she is doing. The book is completely dependent on the author for everything. Most

authors try to give us a sense of the inner urgency of
what they are writing, and claim that the movement of
the book is often out of their hands. This is a sense that
Gertrude Stein as her own narrator is at great pains not
to give us. *The Making of Americans* is totally a product
of Gertrude Stein and depends on her completely for its
pace, which she speeds up or slows down at will.

The narrative method of this book contains other
peculiarities than digressions and authorial comment
that give it its abstract character. One characteristic is
the withholding of information. Of the three governesses
of the Hersland children, Miss Stein tells us the name of
only the third, Madeleine Wyman. We know that Mr.
Hersland was a butcher in the old country and we know
that he becomes a rich man in the United States. But
Miss Stein does not tell us how he makes his fortune. She
intimates in the beginning of the book and again at the
end that Alfred Hersland is a dishonest man. But she
never tells us any of the dishonest things that he did. We
have noted her earlier reticence about sexual matters in
"Melanctha," but here we are dealing with more than
reticence. The withholding of information is a definite
part of the narrative style of *The Making of Americans*.

Related to this are her repeated promises throughout
the book to tell us the story of some one. She constantly
prepares us for what she proposes to do next. "This is
now a history of Martha Hersland. This is now a history
of Martha and of everyone who came to be of her living." (290) Whereupon we are made to wait for about
100 pages before the story of Martha Hersland actually
begins. Whenever she promises us a "history" she always
gives us one, but she does it when she is ready and she

will make us wade through digression after digression until such time.

There are times, however, when Gertrude Stein's lack of concern for the traditional storytelling methods leads her to do something almost the reverse of the withholding of information. She will tell us how something will turn out even before she begins telling us the story.

Alfred Hersland married Julia Dehning. They were not successful together in their married living, this is to be now a complete history of them and of every one connected with either of them. (602)

One of the traditional methods of maintaining a reader's interest in a story is to keep him guessing as to how things will end. But Miss Stein denies us even this in most instances. Not only that, but she rarely gives us the reasons why things happen. After preparing us for the imminent break-up of the marriage of Alfred and Julia she then gives an accounting of their personalities and tells us a few of the events of their married life; but nowhere does she give the clues to the reasons for their incompatibility. Nor does she analyze the reasons for the unsuccessful marriage of Martha Hersland and Philip Redfern. She gives us the personalities of each of her people and lets us draw our own conclusions. It is the individual consciousness and personality that is important, not the relationship.

Another part of Miss Stein's narrative technique that adds to the scientific character of the book is her use of definition. She first defines her terms, and then, once having done so, she uses them throughout the rest of the book without repeating the definition.

There are then two kinds of women, those who have dependent independence in them, those who have in them independent dependence inside them; the ones of the first of them always somehow own the ones they need to love them, the second kind of them have it in them to love only those who need them, such of them have it in them to have power in them over others only when these others have begun already a little to love them, others loving them give to such of them strength in domination. (165)

Many women have at some time resisting in them. Some have resisting in them as a feeling of themselves inside them. In some kinds of women resisting is not a feeling of themselves to themselves inside them. In some kinds of women resisting can only come from such a feeling. This makes two different kinds of women and mostly all women can be divided so between them. (166)

Having made her definitions, Miss Stein feels free to use them throughout the rest of the book. For instance:

Quarrelling is not letting those having attacking be winning by attacking, those having resisting being be winning by resisting, those having dependent being be winning by dependent being, those having engulfing being be winning by engulfing being. This is quarrelling in living, not letting each one by some one be winning by the being in them. This is certainly quarrelling in living. There is a great deal of quarrelling in living, that is reasonably certain and that is a very natural thing as certainly very many are not winning with the being in them. (666)

In addition, Miss Stein uses these terms in connection with most of the characters in the book. Themes and terms are defined and then are always available to the author, and they may rise to the surface of the narrative at any time.

Perhaps the most celebrated aspect of the narrative

method of *The Making of Americans* is Gertrude Stein's use of repetition. This manifests itself in a number of ways, among them repetition of syntactical patterns, themes, and characterization. One of the most obvious forms of repetition that Gertrude Stein uses is her habit of redefining the nature of her book. Periodically she will stop what she is doing and make a statement that always begins, "This then is a history of . . ." This form of repetition arises from Gertrude Stein's narrative method, which allows her to digress as long as she likes. As a result, she constantly feels the need to reiterate or perhaps even to rediscover for herself the nature of her book whenever she comes back from the midst of digression.

Another form of repetition related to the above is her constant "beginning again." Most often she returns from a digression with the phrase, "as I was saying." With this she begins again where she left off before her digressing. Perhaps the constant stops and starts, pausing and beginning again, mirror the struggle of the bottom nature of the individual consciousness to express itself.

Her repetitions of themes take two forms. The first is the fastening on and repeating of a theme again and again in a short space of pages:

There have been always many millions made just like the mother and the fatter sister Sophie Shilling. That is, there have been always many millions made just like them if they really have nothing queer inside them. Perhaps they have something queer inside them that makes them different from the many millions who have been made just like them. (81)

Then on the following three and a half pages she talks about everything in terms of "queerness." After this, she drops the term.

The second form of thematic repetition is similar to the repetition of defined terms that we discussed earlier. It is more like the repetition of a *motif* that runs throughout the lives of her characters. The enigmatic, older Mr. Hersland takes his family to Gossols and buys a house and land in a section in which no one of his means or social class lives. Gertrude Stein refers to this as "the ten acre place in the part of Gossols where no other rich people were living." This *motif* is repeated again and again, especially in relation to the Hersland children who develop a genuine sense of alienation from having to live so far out of the sphere of their social class.

In addition, the Stein style becomes increasingly molded around syntactical repetition. Her use of repetition with variation is her attempt to capture the effort of the bottom nature of the individual consciousness to make itself known. In one of her *Lectures in America* she tells us of this attempt.

I then began again to think about the bottom nature in people, I began to get enormously interested in hearing how everybody said the same thing over and over again with infinite variations but over and over again until finally if you listened with great intensity you could hear it rise and fall and tell all that that there was inside them, not so much by the actual words they said or the thoughts they had but the movement of their thoughts and words endlessly the same and endlessly different.[14]

Rather than discuss this in general terms, let us turn to a passage of her prose in the repetitive manner and analyze the components of the style.

[14] P. 138.

Some one having some one who was with them become a dead one could be saying, when some one was saying something, that one does not know he is a dead one, he will never know that thing. He does not know he is a dead one, some one said of some one who was a dead one. Some one could be certain that some one who is a dead one would not know he was a dead one, some one could not know that some other one who was a dead one would not know that that one was a dead one. Some one then has been quite certain that some one who was with them when that one was a dead one did not know then that that one was a dead one. Some have been certain that every one who is a dead one does not then know that that one is a dead one. (724)

The immediate reaction to a passage such as this one is that it is merely a series of sentences talking about the same thing. The statement is partially true. All of the sentences are about the same thing; they even have a series of phrases in common. However, within the set pattern of what each of the sentences has to say is a syntactic variety that gives the paragraph its unique character.

The first sentence presents quite a bit of information. There are two people in the scene, and a third person has died ("become a dead one"). When one of the two living ones is talking, the other living one could say that when one is dead he (the dead one) can never know it. The thought seems self-evident. In the next sentence Gertrude Stein presents the same thought stripped of all the other descriptive baggage of the preceding sentence. Some one is talking of another person who is dead. The speaker says that the dead person does not know that he is dead. Miss Stein then examines the same thought from still another angle. One can be certain that someone who was dead would not know that he was dead; but one could not know that another dead person would not know that the first dead person was dead. (I am not concerned with either the truth or logical consistency of her statements.) The fourth sentence tells us that in the past some one has been certain that a dead person who was with him did not know that he (the dead person) was dead. And from the fifth and final perspective: people have been certain that a person who is dead does not know that he is dead.

It should be obvious that although the thought content of the paragraph is quite simple, there is a great deal of variety within the patterns of the repetition. In five different ways Gertrude Stein insinuates substantially the same thought into our minds until, if we concentrate on what she is doing, we can hardly forget what she has to say. Whether or not what she has to say justifies all of her effort (and ours) is not relevant to our present considerations. Although each of the sentences is a repetition substantially of the one previous, Miss Stein has each of the sentences do something just a bit different from that of its predecessor. Therefore, the thought, though the same, is different each time. This basic pattern can be followed in almost all of Gertrude Stein's characteristically repetitive paragraphs in *The Making of Americans* and in the books that follow (as we shall see), whether the paragraph contains three sentences or thirty. There is an interlocking progression in thought from the first sentence to the last, from the particular statement to the general conclusion, weaving its way through the pattern of repetition.

Although the paragraph is usually her major unit of

structure, quite often the repetitive pattern extends across paragraphs. Limitations of space prevent our examining more than one large paragraph at a time, but there are whole sections of *The Making of Americans,* especially toward the end, in which the repetitions run along for pages on the same topic. Miss Stein's way of making units as large as these seem coherent is to introduce into the pattern of repetition a new phrase which seems like excess baggage for a sentence or two, until it assumes a more important part of each succeeding sentence and the important preceding thought is slowly excised.

Repetition is also Miss Stein's main method of characterization. She tells us this herself in many paragraphs of *The Making of Americans.*

Many things then come out in the repeating that make a history of each one for any one who always listens to them. Many things come out of each one and as one listens to them listens to all the repeating in them, always this comes to be clear about them, the history of them of the bottom nature in them, the nature or natures mixed up in them to make the whole of them in anyway it mixes up in them. Sometime then there will be a history of every one. (183)

The key words here are "repeating" and "bottom nature." Life is presented with the implied metaphor of struggle, and the repetition is the embodiment of the struggle of the individual consciousness to make its bottom nature clear to the world. There is also the implication in this paragraph, in the phrase "natures mixed up in them," of the deterministic role of heredity, which we shall discuss shortly.

The characters of *The Making of Americans* differ

from those of the previous two works in that they are even further emancipated from the social context. Although the sub-title of the book is "The History of a Family's Progress," the characters of the book are not a family in an organic sense, but rather the individual members of a family.

> Where the abstracted interiority of Melanctha was seen in dramatic relation to the interiority of Jeff Campbell, the people in *The Making of Americans* are seen as an enormous collection of separate units with almost no active relation to each other. They are fathers, mothers, sons, and daughters well enough, but this is, *to themselves inside them* and to the presentation, a fairly adventitious situation or quality to their separate interior existences.[15]

Although we see the characters in the company of other people, the relationships they form are not important. Miss Stein is interested only in the "bottom nature" of each individual as it expresses itself in repetition.

The group that the individual belongs to is much larger than the family: it is the type. Once again, Gertrude Stein takes a characteristic that she first explores in her article, "Cultivated Motor Automatism," mentions in *Things as They Are,* and develops in *Three Lives,* and takes it much farther than she did in any of the previous writings. All of her characters exemplify certain types of humanity that Gertrude Stein seems to have formulated quite carefully. The older Herslands belong to the old world types that they can never escape even after years in America. "Julia Dehning was now just eighteen and she showed in all its vigor, the self-satisfied crude domineering American girlhood that was strong inside her." (13)

15 Sutherland, *op. cit.,* p. 53.

There is obviously a national type to which the younger generation of both families belong. The poorer people from the Gossols neighborhood in which the Herslands live can never rise from their type to socialize with the Herslands. People can never shed the characteristics of the class of people to which they supposedly belong.

Miss Stein presents her notion of psychological determinism on the very first page:

> It is hard living down the tempers we are born with. We all begin well, for in our youth there is nothing we are more intolerant of than our own sins writ large in others and we fight them fiercely in ourselves; but we grow old and we see that these our sins are of all sins the really harmless ones to own, nay that they give a charm to any character, and so our struggle with them dies away.

We all, as young people, want to change ourselves and others, but as we grow older we realize that not only can the leopard not change his spots, but that the flaws in our personality are those things that give us our character. In other words, we accept our own personalities because there is nothing we can do to change them, and we should not look on this fact with regret.

The notions of heredity with which we became familiar in our study of "Melanctha" appear throughout *The Making of Americans*. Here is a description of Alfred Hersland:

> There was then Mr. Hissen and Mrs. Hissen and Alfred Hersland had it in him to have a good deal in him Mr. Hissen being but it was a very different thing in him this being in him than it was in Mr. Hissen. Alfred never had in him at any time in him religion, he was a mixture then of old Mr. Hissen and old Mr. Hersland who was a butcher when he was a young

man working and who was a man who had important feeling in him from having been a little important then in religion. (512)

Whatever there is to the "bottom nature" of Alfred Hersland is then a product of the combination of father and maternal grandfather. This is something that Alfred Hersland can never hope to escape.

There are other similarities to the abstractionism in "Melanctha" that we might point out. The speeches of the characters are attempts once again at capturing the rhythm of speech rather than an exact transcription.[16] Of course, the instances of dialogue in *The Making of Americans* are extremely rare. Gertrude Stein tells us about moments of dialogue that may have occurred in the past, but she rarely lets us hear two people having a conversation.

Another characteristic that this book shares with its predecessor is the casual way the deaths of the characters are introduced. Here is the death of the oldest Dehning:

He had been left out of all life while he was still living. It was all too new for his feeling and his wife was no longer there to stay beside him. He felt it always in him and he sighed and at last he just slowly left off living. (6)

The Hersland grandmother expires in the following manner:

She was then very old, and always well, and always working,

[16] To those who feel that Gertrude Stein simply had no ear for realistic dialogue, I suggest that they read *Brewsie and Willie,* a series of fictional conversations of American G.I.'s of the Second World War. In this book Miss Stein demonstrates that she indeed had a remarkable sense of the way people sound when they talk.

and then she had a stroke, and then another, and then she died and that was the end of that generation. (42)

The casual attitude toward death is, of course, in keeping with the abstract notions of plot we have already noted throughout *The Making of Americans*. Since even the notion of story is almost done away with, the idea of death as a climax to everything can hardly play a role in such a book. As in the passage from Ecclesiastes, "One generation passeth away, and another generation cometh; but the earth abideth forever" (I:4). The generations of Herslands and Dehnings may pass on, but there will always be people around, and these people will have the bottom natures that their heredity and the type to which they belong have determined.

Gertrude Stein presents her characters as propositions of her notions of human psychology. Usually the proposition comes first as a kind of theorem, and then the character follows as its demonstration.

. . . some have it that they feel themselves inside them as big as all the world around them, some have it that they are themselves the only important existing in the world then and in some of them for forever in them—these have in them the complete thing of being important to themselves inside them. (153)

This is the theorem. Gertrude Stein has described the type, the essence that precedes existence. A short paragraph about "middle living" follows. Then:

David Hersland in his daily living had many things in him. He had his own way of loving. The way a man has of thinking his way of beginning and his way of ending in most of the millions of every kind of men comes more from the bottom nature in him from the way of loving he has in him and that makes his kind of man, other natures are mixed up in him, but mostly his way of loving goes with his way of thinking goes with the kind of practical nature he has in him, goes with his way of working, comes from the bottom nature in him. (154)

Here is the demonstration of the theorem, followed immediately by another digression on the subjcet of psychological types. All the characters are introduced in a similar fashion. There is nothing specifically said to connect the theorem with the demonstration. The relationship is made by the juxtaposition of the two.

Occasionally, the demonstration will precede the theorem; however, the *quod erat demonstrandum* of her character portrayal continues. Even governesses and seamstresses are handled with the same style, and they are often given as much space as the supposedly major characters of the chronicle. They are, after all, illustrative of the poorer social class types. All the characters of *The Making of Americans* fit into a giant abstract, almost geometric, scheme. Miss Stein's is one of the last attempts to reduce all of humanity to a few workable principles, which in her system take their form as psychological types.

Sometime then there will be a complete history of all repeating to completed understanding. Some time then there will be a complete history of every one who ever was or is or will be living. (294)

This was a possibility she really believed in at the time. Her supposed attempt to do this in *A Long Gay Book* was suspended after less than two hundred pages.

Miss Stein's abstractionist concerns extend, as we have seen previously, to her use of vocabulary. In *The Making of Americans* her private use of the English language is carried even further than before, although not nearly as far as it was to be carried a few years later. Her awarding of private meanings to words we examined in "Melanctha." In *The Making of Americans*, often connected with her increased use of the present participle, she substitutes for the standard forms of words or phrases new ones of her own. For "middle age," she uses "middle living." She constantly differentiates between "living" and "being," "being" and "existing." Successively, as I have listed them, each of the words implies a decreasingly active role on the part of the individual in the flow of life. When Miss Stein uses a term such as "human being," she does not use it as the name for a certain kind of living creature, but as the name for a process (that of "being") with which the quality of humanity is associated. The word "human" has the same function in this phrase as the other modifiers in phrases such as "stupid being," "impatient being," and "anxious being" that Gertrude Stein uses to describe her characters throughout *The Making of Americans*. The term "being" here refers to the process of the individual bottom nature in expressing itself.

Occasionally Miss Stein will begin using a word in a peculiar fashion without defining its meaning in any way. Such a word is "important," and the phrase in which it is used is "important feeling" that a person has inside him with regard to something. She begins using this in connecton with the older Mr. Hersland early in the book (page 55). The term and phrase are used continuously until they are finally explained over one hundred pages later.

Being important to one's self inside one. Being lonesome inside one. Making the world small to one to lose from one the lonesome feeling a big world feeling can make inside any one who has not it in them to feel themselves as big as any world can be around them. Being important inside one in religion can help one loose from one the lonesome feeling a big world can give to one. . . .

The important feeling of one's self to one inside one in one's living is to have in one then not anything of such a lonesome feeling. (160)

Here, as before in her withholding of information, Gertrude Stein insists that the reader be prepared to wait until she is ready to divulge her secrets. In order that he have a complete command of her book from page to page, Gertrude Stein demands that the reader have read it a few times.

Gertrude Stein continues to employ the euphemism, although its importance in *The Making of Americans* is only minor. Two of the euphemisms that she carries over from *Three Lives* are "wisdom" and "real experience," which in most instances have the same suggestion that they had in "Melanctha."

What is most obviously abstract about *The Making of Americans,* however, is its style. The liberties that Gertrude Stein takes with the traditional grammar, syntax, and punctuation are probably the greatest that any writer of English had done up to that time. In addition, her language is approaching a point now where it is so stylized that it has a system of patterns that appear in almost every paragraph. A full exploration of the linguistic patterns in the writing of Gertrude Stein and particularly in *The Making of Americans* would require almost book-length documentation. However, an exploration here of a few characteristic patterns and the analysis of a characteristic passage of prose will serve to demonstrate the lengths which Gertrude Stein has traveled on the path to a truly abstract style which she will finally discover in her next works.

For one thing, Gertrude Stein develops into a major feature of her style the use of the present participle that we noticed in a few passages in "Melanctha." Miss Stein's concerns are now so exclusively directed on the process of the individual consciousness in expressing its essence that she speaks of everything in terms of process. Probably more than half her verb forms use some form of the progressive ending. She constantly elevates participles into substantives, and she reduces substantives with participial endings back to participial functions. There is little point to quoting a passage to illustrate this. Almost any passage from the book will serve this purpose, as the already quoted passages show.

The paragraph is the major unit of her prose, as has already been noted by Donald Sutherland, who says that in *The Making of Americans* "each paragraph is made to be a complete interior event."[17] As we have seen in our analysis of the paragraph that illustrated repetition, the sentences had no life of their own. They were important only as rhythmic units in the building up of the effect of the paragraph. One of the difficulties that readers have had with *The Making of Americans* is undoubtedly the fact that while the paragraphs are complete units in themselves, the relationships between them are not nearly as strong as those between her sentences. Often

[17] Sutherland, *op. cit.,* p. 61.

the reader feels himself victimized by what seem to him arbitrary juxtapositions, whose logic is not apparent at first. However, the reader who comes to *The Making of Americans* from the poetry of Pound and Eliot should have little problem in acclimating himself to such difficulties. As in so many modern works, the logic behind the continuity is that of free association or perhaps the stream of consciousness. Since Gertrude Stein is at such great pains to give us the impression that she created her book as she went along, perhaps the metaphor of *The Making of Americans* as a stylized stream of the Stein consciousness is not far off the mark.

Although the sentences in *The Making of Americans* are merely the building blocks of the Stein paragraph, they have within them quite a bit of variety. Indeed, it is within the sentence that Miss Stein does most of her stylistic experimentation. And most of her experiments are designed to cut down the movement of the prose to render it more abstract. An example of this is her use of the parenthetical statement that she habitually installs in the middle of a sentence.

Those men who began beginning with him and then left him to do their own ending, *being afraid of the way of going on with a beginning in him, wanting to be doing their own ending,* these could not be certain in his middle living whether he would be ending his beginning in success or in failing. (472, italics mine)

I have italicized the parenthetical statements that break up the sentence. The sentence is so broken up that Miss Stein gives the main verb of the first clause ("could be") an unnecessary subject ("these"). However, it has been so long since the original subject appeared that Miss Stein feels it necessary to put in another one. The parenthetical statement breaking up the middle of the sentence is one of the recurring patterns in the syntax of *The Making of Americans*.

Still another seeming vagary of the style of *The Making of Americans* is the idiosyncratic punctuation. Miss Stein connects sentences with commas, never uses a semicolon, and uses commas within a sentence only when absolutely necessary or perhaps when she remembers to do so. She treats the subject in *Lectures in America*:

And what does a comma do, a comma does nothing but make easy a thing that if you like it enough is easy enough without the comma. A long complicated sentence should force itself upon you, make you know yourself knowing it and the comma, well at the most a comma is a poor period that it lets you stop and take a breath but if you want to take a breath you ought to know yourself that you want to take a breath. It is not like stopping altogether which is what a period does stopping altogether has something to do with going on, but taking a breath well you are always taking a breath and why emphasize one breath rather than another breath.[18]

If this sounds like the later Stein trying to justify her earlier ignorance, here is an excerpt from an unpublished letter she wrote to Alfred Steiglitz on March 6, 1912, concerning his imminent publication of her portraits of Picasso and Matisse in *Camera Work*:

You will be very careful, will you not, that no punctuation is introduced into the things in printing. It is very necessary as I have put in all of it that I want and any that is introduced will make everything wrong.[19]

[18] P. 22.
[19] Unpublished TLS in Gertrude Stein Collection, Yale Collection of American Literature.

Even less than a year after she finished *The Making of Americans,* Gertrude Stein insisted that her idiosyncratic punctuation had a rational basis. Just how well Gertrude Stein could have followed the traditional rules of punctuation is a matter that we can never really determine; however, what we can assess is the effect of her use of punctuation on the style of this book. We find once again that the punctuation is another element that slows down the movement of the sentence. What Miss Stein forces the reader to do is involve himself in the very act of supplying his own punctuation. Certain passages whose meaning would be made much clearer were they punctuated in the traditional manner require one to supply mentally his own commas, semicolons, periods, and question marks. The reader is forced to do nothing less than become a part of the creative process himself.

Still another of Gertrude's Stein's variation patterns within her sentences is her use of syntactical discontinuity. She jolts the reader by reversing the usual word order. "No, *them* we never can feel as young grown men and women." (6-7, italics mine) Gertrude Stein's way of capturing our attention and emphasizing her point is to place the object of the verb before even the subject and to change the traditional sentence order from subject-verb-object to object-subject-verb. This also has the effect of halting, if even momentarily, the narrative flow. "She loved it in a way the struggle he made each day a new one for her." (26) Had she written this sentence in the kind of Basic English against which we must measure its discontinuity, it might have read something like this: "In a way she loved the new struggle that he made for her each day." Miss Stein disrupts this order by adding the word "it" after the main verb, changing the modifier "new" into a substantive ("a new one") and moving the substantive five words and a clause beyond the place where the traditional modifier would have gone. The simple sound of Gertrude Stein's discontinuous sentences is linguistically quite complex.

There are many other qualities of the style of *The Making of Americans* that we could discuss, such as the use of indefinite words, but the best way to demonstrate what is going on in a given passage of this book is to analyze one. The following is one of the better known sections of *The Making of Americans:*

I am writing for myself and strangers. This is only way that I can do it. Everybody is a real one to me, everybody is like some one else too to me. No one of them that I know can want to know it and so I write for myself and strangers.

Every one is always busy with it, no one of them then ever want to know it that every one looks like some one else and they see it. Mostly every one dislikes to hear it. It is very important to me to always know it, to always see it which one looks like others and to tell it. I write for myself and strangers. I do this for my own sake and for the sake of those who know I know it that they look like other ones, that they are separate and yet always repeated. There are some who like it that I know they are like many others and repeat it, there are many who never can really like it. (289)

The only thing that is perhaps unusual about the opening sentence is the progressive form of the verb. It would ordinarily go unnoticed. I mention it only because Gertrude Stein expresses the same thought a few sentences later in the standard present-tense form. In the first sentence we may assume that Miss Stein means the process of her present writing. In the second sentence

Miss Stein begins her dislocation of traditional English syntax. There are two potential ambiguities in the sentence, "this" and "it." What is the referent of the first word of the sentence? Does it refer to what is said in the opening sentence? If so, then what does the final word, "it," refer to? If both words refer to the same thing, then the sentence goes in a complete circle. If only one of these indefinite pronouns refers to the material contained in the first sentence, then we simply do not have the information to lift the other one out of its ambiguity. What "this" really refers to is "writing for myself and strangers," while "it" refers simply to "writing." Miss Stein could have avoided the ambiguity by writing, "This is the only way that I can write." But she has substituted the vague verb, "do," for the specific one. Also, she has completed a thought that most writers have been trained to leave "understood" by adding "it" to the end of the sentence.

The third sentence presents us with another major characteristic of the style of *The Making of Americans*, the changing of an adjective into a substantive quality. Rather than saying, "Everybody is real," Miss Stein changes "real" into "a real one." The abstract quality becomes even solider. The second part of the sentence following the comma, which is really another sentence, shows only one moderately unusual usage, "too to," which has almost the quality of a pun. The ordinary writer of standard English would have avoided such a repetition of sounds so close together by substituting "also" for "too." Perhaps, too, he would have placed "also" after "is."

"Of them" in the last sentence of the first paragraph is

usually left out of similarly constructed sentences. At any rate, it is redundant and unnecessary to the meaning of the sentence. The word "it" later on has no referent, and shall remain without one until well into the next paragraph. It should normally be followed by a comma. The words "and so" that introduce the last clause imply that what is to follow proceeds logically from what has been said before. However, in this instance the logic behind the statement must remain ambiguous until we discover a few sentences later the meaning of that ambiguous "it."

The first sentence of the next paragraph begins with the vague substantive "every one," and it is written as two words rather than one. There is also a shift in emphasis from the "I" to the general "they." The use of the vague substantive is characteristic of the writing, as we have already seen. In the previous paragraph, "everybody" appeared twice, "some one" and "no one" once each. We shall see more of the same throughout the rest of this second paragraph. In the first clause of the sentence we see once again our ambiguous "it." The second contains the redundant and vague "of them," vague because its plural number would not normally agree with "every one," as Miss Stein wants it to do here. A few words further we find our ambiguous "it" once again, followed finally by an explanation of what it means, "every one looks like some one else," an elaborate way of saying that there are types to which everyone belongs. A comma should appear before the final "and." The following sentence contains nothing of an unusual syntactical nature. It introduces a new way in which "every one dislikes it;" this time they dislike to "hear" it.

The third sentence shifts us back to the "I." It contains a couple of split infinitives. Also, the first "it" of the second clause is unnecessary to the meaning of the sentence and serves merely to slow down the pace once again. The next sentence reiterates the opening *motif* of the first paragraph, and it is followed by a sentence that justifies the repetition of the exact wording of the first sentence and repeats a common *motif* of the book, that of being "separate and yet always repeated." The final sentence adds nothing to our knowledge of Gertrude Stein's snytax that we have not discovered in previous sentences. It is really two sentences separated by a comma.

I have chosen this passage mainly because it is conceptually not a difficult one. Since it is one of the "easy" passages of the book, it should make doubly clear the linguistic complexity that is present in Gertrude Stein's writing, a complexity that shows itself to be discontinous with that of traditional standard English. It is not the complexity of sentences with interrelated compound and complex clauses, or of Latinate words, or of elaborate figures of speech. Miss Stein is beginning to do everything she can to render a semantically thin and syntactically simple style discontinuous with any English writing that has gone before it, static and abstract. Every other phrase, it seems, has some kind of a prose caesura that makes the reader pause or stop altogether until he can put enough of the pieces together to go on to the next set of words. And the style of *The Making of Americans* is only a preparation for what is to follow.

Actually Gertrude Stein takes great pains to prepare us for the works that are to follow. The final section of the book, that with David Hersland as its central figure, becomes increasingly abstract in a number of ways. There occur in this long section almost no events to speak of. We are given nothing other than a series of considerations of the nature of David Hersland and of his type. These are more general and abstract than anything that have gone before because there are no passages of a concrete nature to balance the generalizations. There are only a few characters other than David Hersland who appear at all in this section, and they are merely mentioned. It is almost impossible to see the central figure of this section within a context other than the generalizations on his bottom nature. We learn next to nothing specific about him. Many of the characters in this section go unnamed, and the reader is expected to have enough control over the entire book to know to whom Miss Stein is referring. There is an increased use of indefinite and general words, such as "one" and "some."

In addition, the writing becomes linguistically more abstract. One feels an increasing sense of playing with words. Gertrude Stein is becoming less interested in the sense of what she is sometimes saying.

When he was not at all a very young one sometimes he was with one. Sometimes he was with more than one. Sometimes he was with two sometimes he was with more than two. Sometimes he was with three. Sometimes he was with more than three. Sometimes he was with four. Sometimes he was with more than four. Sometimes he was with five. Sometimes he was with more than five. (854-55)

This is repetition almost for its own sake, and one gets the feeling that what is said no longer matters. It is the words themselves and the sounds they make that are all-important.

In many ways, then, this final section of her largest book looks forward to what Gertrude Stein is to do immediately after it. She has been preparing us for *A Long Gay Book* by her remarks throughout *The Making of Americans*. One or two of the passages in this final section prepare us for *Two*. It is no wonder that these resemblances exist, because if Donald Gallup is correct, she was probably working on both of these books while she completed the end of *The Making of Americans*.

As individual as *The Making of Americans* is, then, we must nonetheless conclude in much the same way as we have in the past: as with its two predecessors, it looks ahead to works that are even more abstract. Without the works that follow it, we would still conclude that this "History of a Family's Progress" is a genuinely abstract work. Having these works as a context, however, we are forced to say that, even with all its abstract qualities, *The Making of Americans* lights the way for the next works that finally cross the line.

5

Portraits and the Abstract Style, 1908-1912

THE YEARS BETWEEN 1908 AND 1912 WERE THE MOST prolific of Gertrude Stein's career. She was working on and off on *The Making of Americans*, which she finally finished in 1911, and at the same time she began a series of works that were ultimately to take her the final step from the repetitive style of *The Making of Americans* to the abstractionism of *Tender Buttons*.

All of the writing of these fecund years has finally been published. The first was *Portrait of Mable Dodge at the Villa Curonia*, in 1912, printed privately by Mabel Dodge. Just after that, two of her portraits saw print in *Camera Work*.[1] Some of the early portraits appeared in 1922 in *Geography and Plays*.[2] Still others were pub-

[1] Short portraits of Matisse and Picasso, since published in *Portraits and Prayers* (New York, 1934), and in *Selected Writings of Gertrude Stein* (New York, 1962).
[2] Four Seas Press (Boston, 1922).

lished in *Portraits and Prayers,* which Random House brought out in 1934 to capitalize on Miss Stein's triumphant return visit to America. Just before this, Alice Toklas had published three of the longer works of this period in *Matisse Picasso and Gertrude Stein.*³ This volume includes *A Long Gay Book, Many Many Women,* and *G.M.P.* Finally, after Miss Stein's death, the Yale University Press published *Two and Other Early Portraits,*⁴ a volume that includes the longer works *Two: Gertrude Stein and Her Brother* and *Jenny, Helen, Hannah, Paul and Peter,* as well as eighteen other shorter portraits from this early period. Except for the first two items mentioned, the rest of the published early portraits exhibit the traditional Stein pattern of being published well after they were written.

With such a mass of material before us we cannot deal with each work in as much detail as we have with the works of the earlier and less prolific years. What we shall do is select two of the longer works to look at in some detail and examine thoroughly half a dozen of the shorter portraits. Most of the works of this period repeat the same techniques, and since we are searching for a pattern and not attempting to treat everything Miss Stein ever wrote, selectivity will serve our purposes best.

The two longer works I have chosen are *A Long Gay Book* and *Two: Gertrude Stein and Her Brother,* because they each exemplify two things: they begin by continuing the style of *The Making of Americans* and end in a new style that exemplifies one of the two major

³ In her Plain Edition of the Writings of Gertrude Stein (Paris, 1932).
⁴ New Haven, 1951.

directions the writing of Gertrude Stein was to take during and after 1908-1912. Almost all the portraits take the direction of either *Two* or *A Long Gay Book*.

A LONG GAY BOOK, 1909-1912

Miss Stein tells us in *The Making of Americans* that she is working on a book that will be "a history of all of them."[5] The book she refers to is *A Long Gay Book*, which she worked on concurrently with the latter part of *The Making of Americans.*

As I say I began A Long Gay Book and it was to be even longer than The Making of Americans and it was to describe not only every possible kind of a human being, but every possible kind of pairs of human beings and every possible threes and fours and fives of human beings and every possible kind of crowds of human beings.[6]

I began to wonder if it was possible to describe the way every possible kind of human being acted and felt in relation with any other kind of human being and I thought if this could be done it would make A Long Gay Book. It is naturally gayer describing what any one feels acts and does in relation to any other one than to describe what they just are what they are inside them.[7]

As it turned out, *A Long Gay Book* was abandoned by the time it reached a small fraction of the length of its predecessor. One coming to *A Long Gay Book* without knowing it is incomplete would not think it a fragment. It begins in the same style we noticed throughout most

[5] Paris, 1925, p. 479.
[6] Gertrude Stein, "The Gradual Making of the Making of Americans," *Lectures in America* (Boston, 1957), p. 148.
[7] *Ibid.*, p. 150.

of *The Making of Americans.* What makes it an important document in the career of Gertrude Stein, however, is that it progressively becomes more and more abstract until in the final pages it becomes almost completely non-representational. The final transition to the abstract style happens before our very eyes. It is no wonder that Gertrude Stein could not go on with *A Long Gay Book.* It is at the end no longer the same book that it was when she began it.

The very intent of *A Long Gay Book* is more abstract than that of *The Making of Americans.* Whereas *The Making of Americans* ostensibly examines the characteristics of types only in relation to the characters that people her book, *A Long Gay Book* sets out to examine all the types possible among human beings and all the various possible combinations of those types. The social context is almost completely done away with. There is no attempt made at any narrative continuity; there is no "story." What we have for 75 per cent of *A Long Gay Book* is a long list of types and their characteristics, names given to certain of the exemplars of the types, and two or more of these names placed together occasionally in a context made almost exclusively of the interaction of their personalities. The characters live nowhere, have no homes, do no work. There is not even any dialogue. It is a world of pure existence, a world of the interaction of consciousnesses.

To take passages from the first pages of *A Long Gay Book* and place them side by side with passages from *The Making of Americans* would show us almost no stylistic difference between the two books. The interlocking repetitive style is still very much in evidence. The focus is still on the core of each consciousness that gives the character his personality. Miss Stein states her aims early in the book:

> Every one has in them a fundamental nature to them with a kind of way of thinking that goes with this nature in them in all the many millions made of that kind of them. Every one then has it in them to be one of the many kinds of men or many kinds of women. There are many kinds of men and many kinds of women and of each kind of them there are always many millions in the world and any one can know by watching the many kinds there are of them and this is to be a history of all the kinds of them.[8]

As stated, the aims are almost exactly the same as those expressed in many passages of *The Making of Americans*. There is a change in vocabulary, however. Instead of the "bottom nature" of the individual, we are now to focus on the "fundamental nature," obviously the same conceptual entity. The personal nature of the book is just as strong as in the previous one, where all the characters are supposedly based on people whom Miss Stein knew or with whom she grew up. Here she goes even further. She gives her "characters" the names of her acquaintances, including her brother Michael, Paul Claudel, Fernande Olivier and others. The book is hardly a *roman à clef*, however.

The nature of the narrator is largely the same as it was in *The Making of Americans*. Miss Stein gives instructions to her readers: "In this book there will be discussion of pairs of people and their relation, short sketches of innumerable ones . . ." (17) She then lists the pairs, most of which do not get dealt with in the book, as it turns out. She also gives directions to herself:

> Then going completely in to the flavor question how persons have the flavor they do there can be given short sketches of Farmert, Alden, of Henderson and any other man one can get having very much flavor and describing the complications in them one can branch off into women . . . then describe Pauline and from Pauline go on to all kinds of women that come out of her . . . Then start afresh with Grace's group, practical, pseudo masculine. Then start afresh with Fanny and Helen and business women, earthy type, and kind of intellect. Enlarge on this and then go back to flavor, to pseudo flavor, Mildred's group, and then to the concentrated groups. (18)

We are still touring the creative process with the author. Miss Stein has dispensed completely by this time with creating any illusion of external reality. Reality consists for her only in the conceptual types of personality and their interactions on one another. If the narrator (Miss Stein) gives herself or the reader instructions, she is no longer tampering with the narrative flow. The only flow remaining here is that of the ideas and theories of the author. Exclusive of style, *A Long Gay Book* takes on the character of a textbook on psychology, not a novel, and the narrator has as much right to interpose herself as the author of a textbook.

Although for most of the early part of *A Long Gay Book* we are struck by its similarities to *The Making of Americans,* such as the use of the abstract generalization, the present participle, and repetition, we see early evidences of Miss Stein's straining at the bounds of this (for her) old style. We see, for instance, many examples of the kind of repetition we saw hints of at the end of the previous book, in which the sense of progressive change and the looking at the same situation from various perspectives are gone. Now we have repetition on a much more simplistic, uncomplex level. Words begin to be repeated almost as carriers of mere sound.

> Coming to be anything is something. Not coming to be anything is something. Loving is something. Not loving is something. Loving is loving. Something is something. Anything is something. (11)

A long stretch of the story continues with capitulations of the various types, all described in the very generalized participial style to which we have become accustomed. After a time Miss Stein begins including names in her descriptions. The names are just that. They do not attach themselves to real people in the context of the action or even the description of events. But they do take somewhat of the abstract edge off the generalized typological descriptions by giving them a peg in the world outside of Miss Stein's conceptualized generalizations. When names are not being used, Gertrude Stein is forced to use words such as "anyone," "everyone," and "some one" to refer to people. Here is an example of a name being attached to a type:

> Boncinelli in being one was the one explaining that he knew what he was saying. He did know what he was saying. He did know that knowing what one is saying is something having meaning. (53)

In terms of meaning in the context in which this passage appears, "Boncinelli" could just have easily been "any one." Even names at this point can do very little to lift *A Long Gay Book* out of the abstract.

Occasionally in the midst of the generalizing in the early part of the book, Miss Stein gives in to the spirit of word play that is to overtake her later. In the following instance we see the word "day" repeated insistently for no ideational reason. Interspersed with it is the phrase "that is to say," whose function, aside from disrupting slightly the syntax of the sentence, is to rhyme with "day."

Each day is every day, that is to say, any day is that day. Any day is that day that is to say if any day has been a day there will be another day and that day will be that day. (36)

Here is another passage in which the rhyme plays among the participial endings and the words "thing" and "something."

A thing being a thing that is that thing, a thing being a thing, a thing having been put down a thing being something and putting down a thing is a thing that is happening and then the thing put down being then that thing, a thing being that thing, a thing is something and a thing being something, a thing being that thing is then that thing and being then that thing it is a thing and being a thing it is that thing and it is then that thing, it is then that thing. (48-9)

Throughout all of this, the charting of types continues, and on every page new names are allied with the generalizations, names such as Vrais, Clellan, Mayman, Watts, and Donger. The only name that crops up continually is that of Clellan, and yet our picture of him never becomes any more concrete than that of any of the other names.

Toward the end of *A Long Gay Book* the paragraphs begin to get much shorter. Throughout the book they have been much shorter on the average than those of *The Making of Americans,* but now they are rarely longer than three sentences. By page 81, sense is beginning to disappear from the sentences. In the following example, the logical connections among "falling," "river," the size of the river, "hearing enough sounds," "little things" which are "scattered" and which "come together" are almost nonexistent.

> Falling is not easy and it is not easy when there is a river that is bigger than it is where it is smaller and it is not easy when there are ways of hearing enough sounds that make all the little things come together who were scattered until they were called. Falling is not easy. (81)

Color and rhythm begin to enter the meaningless sentence and paragraph:

> A tiny violent noise is a yellow happy thing. A yellow happy thing is a gentle little tinkle that goes in all the way it has everything to say. It is not what there was when it was not where it is. It is all that it is when it is all that there is. (82)

What Miss Stein does in sentences and paragraphs such as the above looks forward to what she is to do in much of her work from now on. The sentence retains the traditional structure of English syntax, but within that framework the semantic structure breaks down. The sentence does communicate what we expect, but the logical connections that we await are never made. We are presented with a structure that we have come through many years of habit to expect to give us a certain pattern of meaning. And then within this structure we are presented with words that make no logical connection at all. The following sentence is structured in such a fashion— "If . . . , then . . ."—that we expect the supposition made in the first clause to be followed by a logical conclusion from the supposition in the second clause: "If stumbling is continuing then a side-walk is restoring." However the logical connection between the clauses does not exist. We look to the following sentences in the paragraph to clear up the mystery.

> If a side-walk is restoring then eating is satisfying. If eating is satisfying then undertaking is beguiling. If undertaking is beguiling then shooing concentrating. If shooing is concentrating then resounding is destroying. That is the way to sleep. (85)

On the surface, these sentences promise to solve the ambiguity. Each one uses the main verb of the final clause of the preceding sentence in its own opening clause. This implies a logical connectiveness between the sentences. But the only things that are logical about this paragraph are its implications. Every suggestion in each of the clauses may be quite possible, but the possibilities do not extend from clause to sentence or from sentence to sentence. There is no reason for all the disparate ideas in the paragraph except that Gertrude Stein put them there. And the conclusion, "That is the way to sleep," has nothing to do with the rest of the paragraph, except that it appears in the same unit with the rest of its sentences. And on top of all this, the paragraph has no logical relationship to the other paragraphs that appear both before and after it on the same page. Miss Stein has finally succeeded in rendering not only the content of her writing, but also the style abstract.

The book proceeds, and the paragraphs become shorter and even more terse:

> Pale pet, red pet, pink pet, blue pet, white pet, dark pet, real pet, fresh pet, all the tingling is the weeding, the close pressing is the tasting. (97)

Even in the structure of the sentence there is less suggestion of meaning. We have here merely the repetition of
"pet" with modifiers toward a *non sequitur* conclusion.
This example, if anything, is even more abstract than the
previous one.

At this point, where meaning has so utterly been abolished, Gertrude Stein now turns to the sounds of words
for her effects. Here is what amounts to a short prose
poem:

> Pardon the fretful autocrat who voices discontent. Pardon
> the colored water-color which is burnt. Pardon the intoning of
> the heavy way. Pardon the aristocrat who has not come to stay.
> Pardon the abuse which was begun. Pardon the yellow egg
> which has run. Pardon nothing yet, pardon what is wet, forget
> the opening now, and close the door again. (100)

The poetic effects include rhyme, rhythm, assonance,
dissonance, and repetition. Miss Stein is beginning to use
words as plastic elements in creations that have no iconic
relationship to anything conceptually recognizable in
the external world. The paragraph is discontinuous with
the other related structures in the book, and the units
within the paragraph are related by nothing more than a
common community of repetitious sounds. The Stein
style that has given and still gives readers more trouble
than any other style conceived by a writer of English has
finally been reached.

The poetic effects continue with this little play on off-
rhymes:

> A lovely night to stay awake and small the cake and
> masticate. A lovely night and no need of surprises, that is what
> makes it so free of noises. (107)

One could choose quotations such as the last few at random from the final pages of *A Long Gay Book* without much variance in kind and quality. Miss Stein has long since given up her original notion of the book as a history of "every possible kind of human being" (3) and is now lost in the world of words that becomes the source of materials for the creation of her abstract world.[9] The last three pages of the book are full of discontinuous paragraphs of one or two sentences. All of the associations and continuity are formed by sounds.

> Notes. Notes change hay, change hey day. Notes change a least apt apple, apt hill, all hill, a screen table, sofa, sophia. (115)

Sounds dictate the puns and the rhymes which people this paragraph. The shiftings in sound from word to slighty different word have something of the quality of a children's game played while bouncing a ball, a game in which the sense of the words is utterly subordinate to the sounds. If primitivism in writing includes the return to the mentality and perceptions of a child, then this paragraph is an example of a primitive style in writing.

The book ends in a seven-line series of *non sequiturs* full of poetic devices and plays on sounds and words.

> Frank, frank quay.

[9] Here is a statement made by Gertrude Stein in "American Language and Literature," a manuscript in the Yale Collection of American Literature that has yet to be published in English. She is speaking of her feeling at the beginning of the twentieth century of liberation from the tired language of the previous age:

> I found myself plunged into a vortex of words, burning words, cleansing words, liberating words, feeling words, and the words were all ours and it was enough that we held them in our hands to play with them; whatever you can play with is yours, and this was the beginning of knowing; of all Americans knowing, that it could play and play with words and the words were all ours all ours.

Set of keys was, was
Lead kind in soap, lead kind in soap sew up. Lead kind in
so up. Lead kind in so up.
Leaves a mass, so mean. No shows. Leaves a mass cool will.
Leaves a mass puddle.
Etching. Etching a chief, none plush. (116)

In the first line appears the pun on "frankly." In the
second line the word "keys" picks up the rhyme with
"quay." There is also the repetitious use of final conso-
nance. The third and fourth lines use the opening repetition of "lead kind" three times and play on the sound of
"soap": "sew up," "so up." The following two lines use
alliteration (repetition of "m" sound) and off rhyme
("cool will" and "puddle"). The final line uses more
repetitive devices in repeating the "tch" sound and soften-
ing it at the end to "sh." A number of the portraits use
this very technique.

A Long Gay Book, then, sets the scene for a number of
different techniques that we shall examine in the portraits of the same period. As with every work of Gertrude Stein's early career, it combines both its qualities
as an individual work and its importance as a transitional
bridge from an earlier to a more abstract stage. However, the transitions from here on become much less
dramatic. There will be few traits in the portraits that
will advance us much technically over what has already
been done in *A Long Gay Book.*

The other two long stories that appear in the same
volume with *A Long Gay Book* add little to the abstract
style of Gertrude Stein, but they deserve some mention
as examples of works of this period. *Matisse Picasso and
Gertrude Stein* (or *G.M.P.*) was written in 1911-1912,

just after the completion of *The Making of Americans,* and it begins in the style of the earlier book. One immediate advance that it makes in the direction of abstractionism is the elimination of names. The heroes of the book are referred to only by pronouns. After a very short time the style moves to that of the later *A Long Gay Book.* The styles of *The Making of Americans* and the latter part of *A Long Gay Book* alternate after this throughout the rest of the book. There is more iconicity in *G.M.P.* Even without the names of the painters we are able to recognize some of the problems of color and form that Miss Stein attempts to render. However, in terms of the abstract style, *G.M.P.* does not go nearly as far as *A Long Gay Book,* and it presents nothing new that we must look for in the portraits.

Many Many Women (1910), like *G.M.P.,* has no names at all in it. The heroines of the book are called "she." It is similar in style to *Two, The Making of Americans,* and the first two-thirds of *A Long Gay Book,* descending into abstractionism only to the point of giving up the interlocking repetitive style for a repetition that repeats for the sake of the sound of the words. At no time, however, does Miss Stein in this book give up meaning. The following passage is as abstract a paragraph as appears in *Many Many Women:*

> Any one liking is intending is not intending. Any one not liking is intending is not intending. Any one liking, any one not liking is not intending, is intending. (197)

TWO: GERTRUDE STEIN AND HER BROTHER

Two: Gertrude Stein and Her Brother, written in 1910-1912, does not go as far toward the abstractionism of *Tender Buttons* as does *A Long Gay Book*. There are few passages that forsake the sense of meaning in the language. The repetitions almost never fail to advance the story conceptually, and there is something of a "story." Although no names appear in the text, we are constantly aware that the book is about someone. It has considerable iconicity when compared to *A Long Gay Book*. The value of *Two* for us lies primarily in the fact that it prepares us for the style of the early portraits.

The story that *Two* tells is of the relationship of Gertrude Stein and her brother Leo, and all the passages of the tale focus directly on the story. There are no sections of generalization about the psychological types to be demonstrated. If Gertrude and Leo Stein exemplify the characteristics of particular psychological types, the author never tells us directly. It is a fact we must divine by implication.

The book is very personal, and to follow what is going on one would do well first to read a biography of its subjects. Even with the biographical knowledge at hand, one is able to recognize the events to which Miss Stein alludes in only the most general terms. The biography is not followed through events that demonstrate the development of the relationship; rather, the action is completely internal. We are witness to shifting states of mind. There is no social context whatsoever. We never see the famous Rue de Fleurus apartment, any of the Renaissance furniture, or modern paintings on the walls. The crowds of artists and friends never make their appearance, and in their occasional effect on the lives and mental states of the principals we see them referred to as "they." We recognize the advent of Alice B. Toklas by the appearance of another "she."

The central concept of personality in this book is the "sound" that comes out of the individual. This is analogous to the "bottom nature" of *The Making of Americans* and the "fundamental nature" of *A Long Gay Book*. This *motif* is presented in the first line of the book, "The sound there is in them comes out from them," and appears in every paragraph from there through page 64, whereupon we begin to have some passages without this form. "Sound" periodically returns from there to the end of the book.

The structure of *Two* is quite simple. Sections in which each character is the central figure alternate, although Miss Stein seems to get a bit more attention than her brother. However, her treatment of a situation that was relatively bitter in actuality is comparatively free from partisanship. She begins the book by attempting to show both the similarities and contrasts of the two of them.

> They are very much alike. They both have sounds coming out of them. They are alike. They both of them have sounds coming out of them that have too much meaning for the ending that is sounding out from them. They are alike. They both of them are not knowing the beginning and ending in sound coming out of them. They are alike. They certainly are very much alike.
>
> They certainly are not at all alike. One of them is hearing himself and is having then sound come out of him. One of them is hearing some one and is then having sound come out of her.[10]

Leo is developed as the cool thinker and Gertrude as the

[10] Gertrude Stein, *Two: Gertrude Stein and Her Brother* (New Haven, 1951), pp. 2-3. In this section of the chapter page numbers in the text refer to this edition.

expressive one. In the beginning he seems to dominate, but slowly she begins to take over control. The coming of Alice Toklas seals the ending of the relationship.

> She said that she knew that she had what she did have when she had had come the one who came and was sorry she came. She said that she knew that the one who had come would feel what she would feel when she was where she was. She said that she would change what she saw would not be changed when she would need what she could see could not be needed. (99)

By the end of the book Leo Stein has been dispossessed, "He could stay and he did stay, he did stay away," (141) and his sister has emerged the stronger: "She was not waiting. All she won was that victory." (142)

From the quoted passages it is obvious that the style of *Two* derives from *The Making of Americans,* minus the passages of abstract generalization. The participles and the closely knit repetitions that slowly advance the "sound" or the "bottom nature" in the process of its struggle for expression are in the same style as the first 700 pages and more of *Two*'s long predecessor. Even some of the same terms are used, such as "attacking" and "resisting." However, unlike in *The Making of Americans,* Miss Stein is not interested in the definition of her terms. This characteristic is allied with her abandoning the usage of the interpolated generalization. The emphasis in *Two* is more on the story and less on the textbook quality of the psychological demonstration. In this way, *Two* is less abstract than *The Making of Americans.* However, in its total abolition of setting and social context, *Two* goes farther than its predecessor.

In language and the meaning of its smaller syntactical

units, *Two* goes into completely abstract verbiage only a few times.

> He had the alteration of the remaining wagon and he did not then feel that he had the skin that was burning when there was there what came to be there as he went in and out in swimming. He was not analogous. (128)

This is as close as any passage in the book comes to dispensing with sense.

Occasionally, Miss Stein plays with the rhymes of different words, but never do these rhymes interfere with the meaning of the passage.

> He was there tame and he had not any piece of name, he had that repetition. That was not the text of that description. (138)

Two looks ahead to the portraits in a number of ways. First of all, many of the early portraits are personal in the same way as *Two* and presuppose knowledge of the subject. They are understandable only with the biographical information which in their general way they suggest. Secondly, they, like *Two,* use the interweaving repetitive technique over much shorter lengths. We shall call this the "cinema technique" because like the moving picture frames they resemble, each of the sentences repeats most of what has been stated in the previous sentence and adds a very small additional piece of information. And so, as in the moving pictures, we see the changing picture only after a number of the frames flash on the screen in sequence.

Third, the early portraits retain the participial style and the general terms used without definition or referent in the text. The early portraits are miniatures of the full-length style of *Two,* while the later ones adapt the style of the later *A Long Gay Book.*

THE PORTRAITS

Analogies between the arts are one of the sure paths to critical difficulties. That such analogies must be attempted can hardly be avoided, however, when one is confronted with the "portraits," "landscapes," and "still lifes" of this period of Gertrude Stein's writing.

In most previous associations of poets and painters, and in all previous comparisons of their works, identifications and congruencies had for the most part hinged upon similarities in subject matter and attitude. Such comparisons are, perforce, wholly "literary." The subjects and images of paintings, and the philosophies of painters, are discussed in relation to the subjects and images of poems and the philosophies of poets. When the cubists jettisoned subject matter, liaisons between poetry and painting on the old basis were no longer possible. The only course open to literature that would emulate painting was that of contemplating its own structure and image. When the literary content of painting was omitted in favor of the freely conceived mathematical or intuitive exercise of purely plastic values, Gertrude Stein also attempted to drop subject matter in order to concentrate freely upon the "plastic" potentialities of language itself.[11]

In this astute comment, John Malcolm Brinnin has managed to set forth coherently Miss Stein's emulation of painting and what forms it took. Having dropped subject matter, Miss Stein tried to use language plastically in the same way that painters use paint and sculptors use their materials. This analogy will work as long as we

[11] John Malcolm Brinnin, *The Third Rose: Gertrude Stein and Her World* (Boston, 1959), p. 129.

remember that it is a metaphor. After all, the materials of the truly plastic arts can be modeled in such a way as is impossible for the artist to do with words. Whereas the materials of painting and sculpture have physical properties of texture, weight, and color, words are conceptual entities requiring an act of the mind to order them into the representation of some kind of idea. Even letters, like words, are by definition symbolic representations of sounds. The simplest uses of pigment, for instance, such as dabs and lines, do not carry the intrinsic symbolic baggage that the simplest forms of written language bear. We must realize this before we make our analogy.

To say that Gertrude Stein uses language plastically means that she attempts to divest it of its traditional structure of meanings by a variety of devices. What she wanted to do in her emulation of the cubist painters was to develop, exclusive of the inherent symbolic nature of words, a written art form without a mimetic relationship to the external world except through certain suggestive devices. She wanted to reorder reality in the same way that Picasso and Braque fragmented the forms of external objects and painted the fragments on the canvas in a completely unique relationship to one another. In other words, she wanted the painter's freedom to create her own reality, so that her creation would be subject to no conventions other than those she imposed or that it imposed upon itself.[12] Whether this is in any ultimate

[12] The following quotation should make evident just how closely Gertrude Stein equated her writing practices with those of the painters:

I began to make portraits of things and enclosures that is rooms and places because I needed to completely face the difficulty of how to include what is seen with hearing and listening and at first if I

sense possible cannot be answered yet, but it is important that we approach the portraits from the context of what Gertrude Stein was attempting to do.

There are four distinct varieties of portraits from the period before *Tender Buttons,* which I shall treat in the following order: (1) Those that use the interlocking repetition of *Two*—the cinema technique; (2) Those that exemplify the transition we saw in *A Long Gay Book;* (3) Series of *non sequiturs* in which the sentences carry very little sense, and which gain effects mainly by suggestion; (4) Poems using *non sequiturs* and depending predominantly on word play and poetic effects. Certain of the most famous portraits, such as the one of Cézanne and "Miss Furr and Miss Skeene," were written later than this period and cannot be included in our discussion.

The earliest portraits that Gertrude Stein wrote follow the pattern of *Two.* Indeed, all of the shorter portraits published in the same volume with *Two* follow this pattern of interlocking repetition. These early portraits can still be termed representational. Though told in the typical participial style full of unspecific generalization, they tell a story or present a recognizable personality. Of course, the nature of the portraits is extremely personal, and the extent of our understanding of them corresponds in great measure to our knowledge of the subject. Knowledge about a number of the subjects is accessible

---

were to include a complicated listening and talking it would be too difficult to do. That is why painters paint still lives. You do see why they do.

"Portraits and Repetition," *Lectures in America* (Boston, 1957), p. 189.

to any reader of a biography of the author. In these early portraits we may still assume a strong relationship between the title of the portrait and the subject of the actual writing.

One of the most well-known early portraits is the first one of Picasso. There are three repetitive *motifs* that weave throughout the repetitions. The first is stated immediately: "One whom some were certainly following was one who was completely charming."[13] The next two *motifs*, "one working" and "bringing out of himself something," are introduced in the first sentence of the second paragraph: "Some were certainly following and were certain that the one they were then following was one working and was one bringing out of himself then something." These *motifs* are weaved in and out of sentences and paragraphs, dropping on the way bits of information. What he was bringing out of him "was coming to be a heavy thing, a solid thing and a complete thing." He is later seen to be "not one completely working." The thing that he is bringing out is described as solid, charming, lovely, perplexing, disconcerting, simple, clear, complicated, interesting, disturbing, repellent, and very pretty.

However, all this information repeated in a number of different contexts does not tell us anything we can measure in the external world purely on the information given in the portrait. We do not know who it was that was following Picasso. What does Gertrude Stein mean when she says he was charming? What was he bringing out of himself? How can he be working and yet "not ever completely working?" Although the syntax of the por-

[13] *Selected Writings of Gertrude Stein,* ed. and introd. Carl Van Vechten (New York, 1962), p. 333.

trait does not in itself become abstract to the point of losing meaning, we must obviously depend on our external knowledge of the subject to make sense out of the writing. We would not even know from the portrait that Picasso was a painter. Miss Stein has abstracted all specific references that would connect the subject to life in the world of things, places, events, and people. What she has retained are the general and conceptualized descriptions of the meanings of actions. The actions and other specific items are not there, but there is still quite a bit that is recognizable mimetically; and the language other then its stylization poses no problems of meaning.

Another example of the first type of portrait was published originally in *Portraits and Prayers* and entitled "Storyette H. M." The initials probably refer to Henri Matisse.

One was married to some one. That one was going away to have a good time. The one that was married to that one did not like it very well that the one to whom that one was married then was going off alone to have a good time and was leaving that one to stay at home then. The one that was going came in all glowing. The one that was going had everything he was needing to have the good time he was wanting to be having then. He came in all glowing. The one he was leaving at home to take care of the family living was not glowing. The one that was going was saying, the one that was glowing, the one that was going was saying then, I am content, you are not content, I am content you are not content, I am content, you are not content, you are content, I am content.[14]

The story line is much more accessible than in the previous portrait. We know a number of quite specific things about the characters. They are married and one of

[14] New York, 1934, p. 40.

them (the male, as we discover after a few sentences) is "going away to have a good time." The other party obviously does not like it. There are relatively few repetitions ("married," "glowing," "leaving"), and the structure of the sentences is comparatively free from syntactic stylization. Even in this little slice of life, however, we have a relatively abstract portrait. There are no names; there is no setting. We do not know the sex of either of the characters until more than half the story is over. We do not know the meaning of the term "glowing." Why does Miss Stein have her character go through the series of repetitions on the word "content" at the end? The basic situation is an abstract one without the development that would be necessary for our more complete understanding of why the characters act the way they do. Even so, these early portraits are less abstract than those that are to follow.

The second type of portrait follows the pattern of *A Long Gay Book*, in that it begins in the style of *The Making of Americans, Two*, and the first type of portrait, and changes by the end to the kind of linguistic abstractionism we shall rediscover in *Tender Buttons*. The example I shall use for this type of portrait is the "Portrait of Constance Fletcher," which appears in *Geography and Plays*. The portrait begins in a manner to which we have become accustomed.

> When she was quite a young one she knew she had been in a family living and that that family living was one that any one could be one not have been having if they were to be one being one not thinking about being one having been having family living. She was one then when she was a young one thinking about having, about having been having family liv-

ing. She was one thinking about this thinking, she was one feeling thinking about this thing, she was one feeling being one who could completely have feeling in thinking about being one who had had, who was having family living.[15]

It continues in this fashion for a page and a half until a new repetitive strain begins, this one to the effect that "She could be then one being completely loving." After a few paragraphs this motif gives way to her "being one being a completely filled one," and then to her being "completely full." (158) Finally, "She was feeling in thinking in being a full one."

The very next lines of the portrait are:

If they move in the shoe there is everything to do. They do not move in the shoe. (159)

These lines have no semantic relation to either the preceding or the following lines. For the next seven pages the portrait becomes a full-scale improvisation, in which full license is given to word and sound play, rhyme, and rhythmic effects.

Come in and that expression is not that one of waiting. To use a name is not the time that seeing has not been. This is discussion. This obligation. This is the composition. (160)

To face the way that each one does say that they have any day which is clearly not away is to say that the time is not there when the color is not lighter and the hair is not redder. This does not make all there is of any invitation. There is not anything of any such suggestion. (164)

The portrait ends on the following note:

All houses are open that is to say a door and a window and

[15] Boston, 1922, p. 157. The next page numbers to appear in the text refer to this edition.

a table and the waiter make the shadow smaller and the shadow which is larger is not flickering. (165)

The pattern is, of course, one with which we are familiar. The opening is the same as in the repetitive early portraits and the other longer works of this period, but after a time Gertrude Stein dissolves the subject matter that she has established and begins to use words "plastically."

The third type of portrait uses throughout its entire body the *non sequitur* style that arises at the end of the "Portrait of Constance Fletcher." The most famous of all the portraits in this style is the "Portrait of Mabel Dodge at the Villa Curonia."

The days are wonderful and the nights are wonderful and the life is pleasant.[16]

This is its celebrated opening line. From there Miss Stein takes the reader through a series of juxtapositions that have only the logic that their internal linquistic structures create for them. At best, we can see a series of suggestions that may be Miss Stein's attempt to evoke the atmosphere of the Villa Curonia. "Blankets are warmer in the summer and the winter is not lonely." "It is not darker and the present time is the best time to agree." (528) "If the spread that is not a piece removed from the bed is likely to be whiter then certainly the sprinkling is not drying." "Abandon a garden and the house is bigger. This is not smiling. This is comfortable." (529) "A walk that is not stepped where the floor is covered is not in the place where the room is entered." (530)

[16] *Selected Writings of Gertrude Stein,* p. 527. Page numbers in text refer now to this edition.

These suggestions, if that is what they are, appear as juxtaposed *non sequiturs,* however, rather than as a series of statements strung together with traditional linquistic logic. The portrait is full of the kinds of rhyming, punning, and word play that we have seen on more than one occasion. It can perhaps best be compared to a cubist painting, in which the title is not to be taken as anything more than suggestive. We are no longer to look for isomorphic relationships between the title and the subject of the portrait, assuming we admit that the portrait has a definable subject.

Since the "Portrait of Mabel Dodge" is rather long, we will be able to have a better idea of the nature of this particular kind of portrait by quoting in full one of the shorter portraits of this variety that was published in *Portraits and Prayers.* The title of this one is "Mrs. Edwardes."

A little grass. Peal it first it shows clothes that means night gowns hours, loaves, feathers, hours, hours, loaves, feathers, feel hours, some more in, little thing, anything pale letters, principal, principal work show full coal hide, full coal hide in, in last angling that is. The most neat couple of stitches are in opposite coils. This makes me ashamed, in.

Leave off more to let anybody be ashamed to have best spread out in twelve when perfectly cool ice. This is most needful. A little thing water melon willing, a little thing to that.[17]

First of all, assuming that Mrs. Edwardes is indeed the subject of the portrait, we must once again look for suggestive implications as to what her presence really is in the writing. If Mrs. Edwardes is a housewife, then the homely implications of many of the words in the portrait

[17] *Portraits and Prayers,* p. 97. Page numbers now refer to this edition.

might make more sense; i.e., "grass," "night gowns,"
"loaves," "feathers" (feather duster?), "coal," "best
spread," "water melon," and the sentence, "The most
neat couple of stitches are in opposite coils." Perhaps the
sentence, "This makes me ashamed, in," is supposed to
be suggestive of the speech of Mrs. Edwardes. Why the
word "in" is set off by commas is unclear. However, all
of these implications are by no means ascertainable.
Thus, the portrait is conceptually definable only through
the possibilities of suggestions that seem to be in the
associations connected with some of the words.

The painters of the period were constantly doing portraits that depended for whatever iconicity they had on
suggestions that seemed to emanate from the associations connected with fragments scattered throughout the
canvas, much the same as the fragments of Mrs. Edwardes seem to be scattered throughout the portrait that
Gertrude Stein has written. In his *Girl Before a Mirror*,
for instance, Picasso presents us with two figures that are
quite distorted but are still recognizable as female. The
face of the girl looking into the mirror is presented in
both profile and half a full-face. The two sets of round
globes on her body seem to be breasts, and yet which set
are they? The girl's arm seems to extend across her mirror image; but is it really her arm or her image's? The
form is fragmented, though not so much as paintings like
Duchamp's *Nude Descending a Staircase,* and yet the
fragments still suggest very definitely the titled subject,
and the suggestive use of color gives us an opportunity
to interpert the significance of the subject. Both Gertrude
Stein and Picasso minimize or fragment their subject
matter so that the thread connecting the actual portrait with the supposed subject is tenuous at best. How-

ever, what makes Gertrude Stein even more abstract than Picasso is that even if a Picasso portrait carries no suggestion of a subject to the viewer of the picture, it can at least convey a meaningful pattern of colors, forms, and a balanced structure within the painting, which we can for our purposes call texture. The painting can be taken in at a glance, and the absence of subject matter no longer presents a serious disability to the viewer of modern painting. In writing, however, without a subject matter the corresponding textural attributes, such as linguistic and auditory structures, are much less accessible under normal circumstances. Perhaps it is due to the difference between the two media, perhaps merely to the fact that we are trained to appreciate colors and form in a painting and not the corresponding values in subjectless writing; perhaps the difficulty is temporal in that we can take in a painting all at once and must spend time to take in a seemingly subjectless word portrait. The human mind may be less capable of functioning on "subjectless" writing than on "subjectless" painting. Whatever the reasons, Gertrude Stein, when she divorces subject matter from her writing as she does in the fourth set of portrait types, forces the reader who approaches them with an open mind to concentrate his attention almost exclusively on those verbal attributes that we have noticed occasionally in the past, such as punning, rhymes, metrical rhythm, repetition, and idiosyncratic punctuation. Some of these portraits take almost the form of poems.

"Irma"

Land side. Irma.
Irma cake, Irma.

Land side bucket, bucket in stuff.
Irma.
Irma is as estel estelable is estelable in it.
Irma. (96)

The effects here are relatively uncomplex. The word
"Irma" is used as a kind of refrain at the end of each of
the lines. It is set off once by commas, the other times by
periods, perhaps simply to show that in reciting the lines
the punctuation makes no difference. "Land side" appears in the first line as a substantive phrase. In the third
line it is used as the modifier of "bucket," which appears
as the last word of the first phrase of the line and the first
word of the second phrase. In the final line Gertrude
Stein introduces a word of her own creation, "estel," following which she varies the form of the word and repeats the variation. There is use of both rhyme and repetition. Initial rhyme connects lines one and three with
the repeated "land side," while the other lines rhyme
initially with the repeated "Irma." Internal rhyme connects "bucket" and "it."

There is little of suggestion that one could get from
the words. Perhaps "land side" is a pun on "landslide,"
but there is no application that we can make of this. The
title is reflected in the content of the portrait only
through the constant repetition of it. We are faced here
with a piece of writing in which, to all practical purposes, meaning has been excised and which can be approached only through the linguistic texture.

Here is a portrait of Guillaume Apollinaire:

Give known or pin ware.
Fancy teeth, gas strips.
Elbow elect, sour stout pore, pore caesar, pour state at.

Leave eye lessons I. Leave I. Lessons. I. Leave I lessons, I.
(26)

Once again, even though Apollinaire is a well-known figure, as poet, art critic, and pornographer, there is little
that we recognize as relating to the subject even by the
suggestion of a fragment. The texture of this portrait,
however, is much richer than the previous one in
rhymes, puns, and repetition of sounds. The first two
lines contain a series of repeated vowels and consonants,
the *n*'s in "known," "pin," "fancy," the *g*'s in "give" and
"gas," the *s* sound in "fancy," "gas," "strips," the short *i*
in "give," "pin," and "strips," the *a* sound in "ware,"
"fancy," and "gas." There is a possible pun on "ware"
("where") in the first line.

In the second line we see the logic of the structure
dictated by the sounds, as the sound of one word dictates
what the next one will be. The "el" in "elbow" leads to
"elect." The "ou" in "sour" leads to "stout." The combination of the "ou" in "stout" and the resemblance to
"spout" gives rise to the following word "pore," which is
a possible pun on "pour." The same word, "pore," is repeated after the comma, this time modifying "caesar." In
this instance it is rather a gross pun on "poor." "Pour"
appears after the next comma, obviously arising from
"pore," and modifying "state," which is the same word as
"stout," except for the change in the middle vowel sound.
The juxtaposition of "caesar" and "state" is, of course, no
accident.

The last line uses repetition of the words "leave," "lessons," and "I," with the word "eye" used as a pun on the
first person singular pronoun. The idiosyncratic punctuation is another means of disrupting the continuity of the

traditional English sentence unit. Played against the discontinuity in the sentence structure is the repetition of the *l, s, v, n,* short *o,* and long *i* sounds.

In her portraits, then, we see Gertrude Stein going through a progressive march toward greater abstractionism. In the final portraits we discover that the entire unit bears no relation to its supposed subject, creates no continuity of subject of its own, juxtaposes totally unrelated words such as "gas" and "strip," and depends for whatever effects it may have on the textural elements of language itself. One could perhaps read suggestive elements into the portraits of "Irma" and of "Guillaume Apollinaire" that would relate them to their supposed subjects, but this kind of ingenuity would represent as much of a creation on the reader's part as the original portrait was on Gertrude Stein's. It seems to me that the only possible way of approaching these last portraits is as language devoid of meaning in the traditional sense, used "plastically" to gain the kind of effects outlined in the above analyses.

If Gertrude Stein has finally abolished from her writing story, setting, movement, subject matter, analyses, and meaning, it would seem that there is only one thing further that she can do in the way of abstractionism other than ceasing to put letters together into words, words into an order, or merely leaving the page blank. She must shift her gaze away from the world of people completely to focus on things. This is what she does in her next creation, *Tender Buttons,* a series of "still lifes" that are the focus of our attention in the next chapter.

6

Tender Buttons

GERTRUDE STEIN WROTE *Tender Buttons* IN 1913, ON
one of the trips she and Alice Toklas took to Spain. It
was published the following year by the poet Donald
Evans,[1] created a minor stir,[2] and disappeared from the

[1] Claire-Marie Press, New York, 1914.

[2] A typical example of the critical reception accorded *Tender Buttons* appeared in June, 1914, in the *Chicago Tribune:*

> *Tender Buttons* is the most recent product of Miss Gertrude
> Stein, the literary cubist. Miss Stein, an affluent American resident
> in Paris, has been for years the high Priestess of the New Artists,
> the Cubists and Futurists. Her own gyrations with words have been
> printed before, but Privately. *Tender Buttons* is the first volume to
> be vouchsafed the Public.
>   It is a nightmare journey in unknown and uncharted seas. Miss
> Stein's followers believe she has added a new dimension to litera-
> ture. Scoffers call her writings a mad jumble of words, and some
> of them suspect that she is having a sardonic joke at the expense of
> those who profess to believe in her.
>   . . . It is not clear whether 'Tender' of the title means a row
> boat, a fuel car attached to a locomotive or is an expression of
> human emotion . . .

Quoted from Elizabeth Sprigge, *Gertrude Stein: Her Life and Her
Work* (New York, 1957), p. 102.

stalls. Today this is perhaps the most valuable edition of Gertrude Stein's writing. Miss Stein always considered *Tender Buttons* one of her most important works, and when the avant-garde magazine *transition* began to appear in Paris, she convinced Eugene Jolas and Elliot Paul to reprint it in an issue of the magazine.[3] This issue of *transition* is now a collector's item. *Tender Buttons* received its first wide circulation in 1946, when it was reprinted by Random House in *Selected Writings of Gertrude Stein,* which was later released by the Modern Library in 1962.

The development of the abstract style throughout the first ten years of Gertrude Stein's career culminates in a set of "still lifes" in which she finally produces a work of almost sustained abstractionism. The emulation of the techniques of painting leads Miss Stein to dispense with people as the subjects of her portraiture and to turn to objects. Picasso at the time was turning to collage as a means of portraying the fragmented world of things. In *Tender Buttons* Miss Stein attempts her own collage. Her writing now becomes so abstract that it is difficult to talk about it in the context of other works of literature, and we are forced to use the metaphors of painting to describe many of her abstract effects.

Before we plunge into *Tender Buttons,* however, we should make one thing clear. Abstract art, by the definition we have been using, is an impossibility, especially in writing. The complex object that is external reality can never be completely excised in any artistic production. A painter who does away with all form and line in his work must nonetheless use color of some shade between white

3 *transition,* II (Fall 1928), 13-55.

and black. This color is part of the world of our experience and is the potential source of associations in the mind of anyone who approaches the painting as viewer or critic. The sculptor uses materials derived from the world of external reality, and no matter how much or how little stylized form he gives to his object, it must still retain associations of some sort for the viewer. In music, even the silent melodies of John Cage are structured around the expectation of a system of sounds that we associate with the world outside ourselves. Cage has perhaps given us the closest approximation of abstract art, for to be truly abstract a work of art must not exist. It must be silence or a void—and not the illusions of either of these.

The materials of the writer hinder the course of abstractionism even further than those of the sister arts. None of the materials used in the other arts are inherently created for the purposes of communication, but rather are there to serve the expressive purposes of the artist. But written language, which exists independent of performance, as written musical notations do not, is the symbolic representation of speech and is a specific creation intended for verbal communication. To reduce the language to mere syntax without meaning still retains the individual word, whose associations are beyond the control of the artist. To make up new words is still to retain the same letters that went into the makeup of the old words, and the human mind will find in these new words resemblances to old ones. If one abandons letters for mere doodles, then one still runs the risk of having the shapes he creates on the page resemble shapes that are in the experience of the viewer. There is no way to

escape into the world of complete abstractionism other
than to sit silently like a Buddha contemplating.

Now, what Gertrude Stein wanted to do was develop
an art that created its own reality and did not depend on
resemblances to the outer world for its recognition as art
by the reader. That she felt painting had achieved somewhat the ability to create its own reality is evident from
this statement from *Lectures in America:*

> . . . any oil painting whether it is intended to look like
> something and looks like it or whether it is intended to look
> like something and does not look like it it really makes no
> difference, the fact remains that for me it has achieved an
> existence in and for itself, it exists on as being an oil painting
> on a flat surface and it has its own life and like it or not there
> it is and I can look at it and it does hold my attention.
>
> That the oil painting once it is made has its own existence
> this is a thing that can of course be said of anything. Anything
> once it is made has its own existence and it is because of that
> that anything holds somebody's attention. The question always
> is about that anything, how much vitality has it and do you
> happen to like to look at it.[4]

That Miss Stein wants the same relative freedom in her
writing as the abstract painters have had for their art is
strongly implied by the middle sentence of the second
paragraph. Without getting ourselves into the thorny
problems of the mode of existence of the work of art, let
us say that Gertrude Stein's desire to give a piece of
writing "its own existence" is important to us mainly as
an indication of what she held as her objective for works
such as *Tender Buttons,* and not as what we must consider a possibility of her achieving. *Tender Buttons* is not

[4] Gertrude Stein, "Pictures," *Lectures in America* (Boston, 1957),
p. 61.

abstract in the absolute sense that we have outlined, but it is a genuinely abstract work within the limitations of the medium, and it gives the illusion of being even more abstract than it is capable of being. Perhaps if we want to draw an analogy with painting, we could call *Tender Buttons* an example of verbal collage, in that it is an attempted juxtaposition of verbal fragments representing fragments from the world of external reality.

Another example from the critical writings of Gertrude Stein will give us more of an idea of what she was attempting to do in her series of still lifes.

Really most of the time one sees only a feature of a person with whom one is, the other features are covered by a hat, by the light, by clothes for sport and everybody is accustomed to complete the whole entirely from their knowledge, but Picasso when he saw an eye, the other one did not exist for him and as a painter, and particularly as a Spanish painter, he was right, one sees what one sees, the rest is a reconstruction from memory and painters have nothing to do with reconstruction, nothing to do with memory, they concern themselves only with visible things and so the cubism of Picasso was an effort to make a picture of these visible things . . .[5]

This is a useful explanation of the cubists' fragmentation of form, and it will work as an explanation of Miss Stein's method in most of *Tender Buttons*, if we accept the analogy she makes between her writing and painting (and indeed we must, or *Tender Buttons* will remain nothing but a series of unrelated phrases). In a strong reversal from the highly conceptualized vocabulary and stylized perceptions of *The Making of Americans*, Miss Stein attempts to portray a structured reality of seemingly unstructured perceptions of the external world.

[5] Gertrude Stein, *Picasso* (London, 1948), p. 15.

The perceptions she attempts to record are those that the mind registers before memory and perceptual conditioning reorder the elements of perception into the structure we know as reality. This method extends even to her use of words in a manner that often bears no resemblance to how the word was ever before used. In other words, even her use of the language rejects the kind of memory that would force her to order her vocabulary into an organized structure of traditional meanings. All the arts of the period seem to have revolted at once against the traditional ways of structuring reality. In music the old harmonic system gives way to the twelve-tone scale. The painters abandon perspective for the flat two-dimensionalism of Matisse or the fragmented form of the cubists. And the writers try to inject new life into the word by using it in fresh contexts or by forsaking traditional meanings.

The very title of *Tender Buttons* should prepare us for this new artistic universe in which words are wrenched from their old meanings. We are inclined to gloss over words that may be given totally unusual meanings when they are used in familiar contexts. *Tender Buttons* may sound like a reasonable enough title, but who has ever before created such a metaphor? How can a button be tender? No one eats a button, and yet Miss Stein imports the term "tender," usually associated with food, and uses it to modify a button, a hard inedible object usually associated with clothing.[6] We can normally conceive of a soft button or even one that bends, but not a "tender"

[6] My discussion of metaphor derives largely from an excellent article by Morse Peckham, entitled "Metaphor: A Little Plain Speaking on a Weary Subject," *Connotation,* I (Winter 1962), 29-46.

one. And yet, Miss Stein has given the word a fresh meaning by disregarding the old ways in which the word was used; in other words, by forsaking memory. "None of the words Miss Stein uses have ever had any experience. They are no older than her use of them . . ."[7] Behind the hyperbole of this statement lies a useful metaphor, for Gertrude Stein wanted nothing more than to preside over the rebirth of the language.

The sub-title of *Tender Buttons* is "Objects Food Rooms," which corresponds to the three sections of the work. The three subjects of *Tender Buttons*, of course, are the subjects of still lifes traditional to painters, including the cubists, and Miss Stein chooses such homely subjects for much the same reasons as the painters. The subject of *Tender Buttons* must be as unobtrusive as possible so that the emphasis may be placed almost completely on matters of technique.

As the created reality and not the original reality had to be everything in the cubist picture, the original reality had to be as simple and familiar as possible, to contain nothing but a visual interest and even that visual interest as unprejudiced as possible by tradition.[8]

Miss Stein, as with most of the modern painters at this point, rejected anything that smacked of the literary in her still lifes.

There is no way to pin down the style of *Tender Buttons*. In its many fragments it uses almost all the techniques we have previously noted, and it adds a few elements of its own. By and large, however, it uses the style

[7] Laura Riding, "The New Barbarian and Gertrude Stein," *transition*, I (June 1927), 160.
[8] Donald Sutherland, *Gertrude Stein: A Biography of Her Work* (New Haven, 1951), pp. 85-6.

of the *non sequitur*. The textural elements noted in the previous chapter are less in evidence, except for those passages that use poetic effects. There is on the other hand more of a relationship between the title of a fragment and the content of the writing that follows it. This is not to say that in these still lifes Gertrude Stein is giving verbal descriptions of potential paintings. When Miss Stein includes objects, colors, and shapes in her fragments, she does this so that they will merely suggest the presence of a physical object of a certain weight, texture, and color. As the cubist painter includes the fragment of an object along with other discontinuous fragments, so Gertrude Stein uses her sentences and phrases, and sometimes even simple words, to build up through repetition (as the painter does by repeating certain similar fragments in his cubist still life) a suggestion or implication of a physical object or set of objects.

Perhaps the main stylistic innovation is the one sentence structure, which ultimately takes on the character of a definition, as in SALAD:

It is a winning cake.[9]

Here there is no chance to build effect by repetition, which has been Miss Stein's chief technical resource. Nor is there an opportunity to use the poetic effects of rhyme and rhythm to enrich the texture. All we have is the simple juxtaposition of the title and the short sentence. Whatever fresh way we may have of looking at the subject is left almost purely to what we can get out of the juxtaposition Miss Stein makes.

[9] Gertrude Stein, *Selected Writings of Gertrude Stein*, ed. and introd. Carl Van Vechten (New York, 1962), p. 495. All page numbers in the text of this chapter refer to this edition.

The first of the "Objects" is A CARAFE, THAT IS A
BLIND GLASS.

A kind in glass and a cousin, a spectacle and nothing
strange a single hurt color and an arrangement in a system to
pointing. All this and not ordinary, not unordered in not
resembling. The difference is spreading. (460)

First of all, although the meaning of the statements is
enigmatic, Miss Stein gives her still life some representational qualities by the inclusion of a few words that refer
back to the title. The words here are "glass" and "spectacle." "Glass," of course, derives directly from the title.
"Spectacle" in one of its meanings at least implies the use
of "glass." These representational resemblances to the
supposed subject matter supplied by the title, slight
though they may be, are enough to set us looking for
other resemblances. However, Miss Stein fills her still
life with a series of undefined and seemingly unrelated
terms that dissipate most of the potential resemblances
between subject and content and leave us with only the
suggestion of a carafe.

What, for instance, does "kind" refer to? Is it there
only because of the rhyme with "blind?" What about
"cousin?" Does it, perhaps like "kind," simply refer to a
vague category to which a carafe either belongs or is
related? Or, since a carafe is an object connected with
food, is "cousin" really a pun on "cuisine?" Which meaning of "spectacle" are we to apply? Does the "single hurt
color" refer to blindness, and does this refer to "spectacle" or "glass?" If none of these problems have been
placed here intentionally by Miss Stein, then this is even
further proof of the suggestive power of words and of

the inability of even the most self-conscious author to divest them completely of their associative powers.

The next of the objects, GLAZED GLITTER, is the subject of a longer "poem."[10] The first word of this is "nickel," which sets up immediately the suggestion of a tarnished coin to correspond to "glazed glitter." The word "change" appears in the next line, which reinforces our notion of the tarnished coin. After this, interspersed with phrases such as

> There is no gratitude in mercy and in medicine. There can be breakages in Japanese. That is no programme. (460)

appear words that seem to have a connection with "glazed": "cleansing," "glittering," "washing," and "polishing." The same method is used here as in the first still life, and indeed this is the method that Gertrude Stein maintains throughout most of *Tender Buttons*.

Occasionally, though not so often as in some of the previous portraits, Miss Stein will make use of rhyme, adding a spirit of play to her picture, as in DIRT AND NOT COPPER:

[10] That Miss Stein thought of *Tender Buttons* as poetry is evidenced by the following statement from "Poetry and Grammar," one of the *Lectures in America, op. cit.,* p. 235.

> And then, something happened and I began to discover the names of things, that is not discover the names but discover the things the things to see the things to look at and in so doing I had of course to name them not to give them new names but to see that I could find out how to know that they were there by their names or by replacing their names. And how was I to do so. They had their names and naturally I called them by the names they had and in doing so having begun looking at them I called them by their names with passion and that made poetry, I did not mean it to make poetry but it did, it made the Tender Buttons, and the Tender Buttons was very good poetry it made a lot more poetry, and I will now more and more tell about that and how it happened.

Dirt and not copper makes a color darker. It makes the shape so heavy and makes no melody harder.

It makes mercy and relaxation and even a strength to spread a table fuller. There are more places not empty. They see cover. (464)

The rhyme here is the repeated *er* ending: "copper," "darker," "harder," "fuller," "cover." In addition, the first line gives the hint of a strong rhythm that Miss Stein then discontinues.

In A BOX we see the use in miniature of the technique of *A Long Gay Book*. The still life begins with the repetition of a series of quite accessible statements about boxes:

A large box is handily made of what is necessary to replace any substance. Suppose an example is necessary the plainer it is made the more reason there is for some outward recognition that there is a result.

A box is made sometimes and them to see to see to it neatly and to have the holes stopped up makes it necessary to use paper. (465)

After this, the writing becomes progressively more abstract and suggestive, until the final paragraph reads

An increase why is an increase idle, why is silver cloister, why is the spark brighter, if it is brighter is there any result, hardly more than ever. (465-46)

At this point there is no longer even a suggestion of the supposed subject.

A LONG DRESS shows the structure of the still life obeying a different kind of logic. The opening sentence is in the form of a question. There is then a series of questions that simply follow the lead of the first question. Here we find that the structural logic of the entire still life is formed by following repetitively the structure of the opening sentence.

> What is the current that makes machinery, that makes it crackle, what is the current that presents a long line and a necessary waist. What is this current.
> What is the wind, what is it.
> Where is the serene length, it is there and a dark place is not a dark place, only a white and red are black, only a yellow and green are blue, a pink is scarlet, a bow is every color. A line distinguishes it. A line just distinguishes it. (467)

The last two sentences are in the form of answers to the preceding questions. But, of course, they are very murky answers indeed, if at all.

After a time the still lifes begin to get shorter, depending less on the relationship, or lack thereof, between sentences and more on the suggestiveness or juxtapositions of words, as in A PETTICOAT:

> A light white, a disgrace, an ink spot, a rosy charm. (471)

All four items in this short catalogue could possibly be associated in some way with a petticoat, but the associations must be made by the reader.

Some of the "poems" are even shorter and more terse. For example, PEELED PENCIL, CHOKE:

> Rub her coke. (476)

In this instance Gertrude Stein is punning on the word "rubber," which we may associate with the rubber eraser on the "peeled pencil." In addition, we have the play on the rhyme of "choke" and "coke." Merely by the dropping of the letter "h" she produces another word of such a different meaning, although both are perhaps associated with the gullet. If the punning implication is correct, then we are faced in "rubber coke" with a metaphor just as startling as the metaphor of tender buttons. But if Matisse can paint a woman with a green nose, why then can't Gertrude Stein write about a rubber coke?

The final "Object," THIS IS THIS DRESS, AIDER, presents us with something relatively rare in the writings of Gertrude Stein, the creation of neologisms.

Aider, why aider why whow, whow stop touch, aider whow, aider stop the muncher, muncher munchers.

A jack in kill her, a jack in, makes a meadowed king, makes a to let.

The words "aider" and "muncher," although used completely out of their ordinary contexts are nonetheless still words that appear in the English language. But the word "whow" is a creation of her own. Miss Stein's abstractionism rarely led her to take this step. In addition, we can see another growing attribute of her abstract style in the changing of the traditional function of English words according to their position in the syntax of the sentence. The verb "kill" appears in the sentence after the preposition "in." Ordinarily, we expect substantives to be the objects of prepositions. However, in using language "plastically" Miss Stein exercises her privilege of using a verb in a different function. The infinitive "to let," which ends this section of *Tender Buttons,* appears as the object of a verb and is modified by the article "a." Only substantives are ordinarily modified by articles, but once again Miss Stein puts the words into the order she desires, not that dictated by the traditional usage of language as an instrument of verbal communication.

The second section of *Tender Buttons,* "Food," is constructed in much the same way, with a title in capital letters followed by a fragment ranging from one sentence to a few paragraphs, except for a few longer specimens which open the section. The first of the food still lifes, ROASTBEEF, covers five pages and is by far the longest of all the *Tender Buttons* fragments, except for the final "Rooms." It begins much like a passage from *Two*, but before the paragraph is complete the style is already the suggestive obscurity we have come to associate with *Tender Buttons*.

> In the inside there is sleeping, in the outside there is reddening, in the morning there is meaning, in the evening there is feeling. In the evening there is feeling. In feeling anything is resting, in feeling anything is mounting, in feeling there is resignation, in feeling there is recognition, in feeling there is recurrence and entirely mistaken there is pinching. All the standards have steamers and all the curtains have bed linen and all the yellow has discrimination and all the circle has circling. This makes sand. (477)

Only "reddening," in the second line, has anything possibly to do with roast beef, and we usually associate "reddening" with the inside rather than the outside of a roast. The first of our really strong suggestions appears two paragraphs later:

> The change the dirt, not to change dirt means that there is no *beefsteak* and not to have that is no obstruction, it is so easy to exchange meaning, it is so easy to see the difference. (477-78, italics mine)

From there on are numerous references to food such as "toast," "chickens," and "tea," but our next reference to beef comes two pages later: "Why should ancient lambs be goats and young colts and never beef . . ." (480) And finally, half a page later we see:

Please be the beef, please beef, pleasure is not wailing. Please beef, please be carved clear, please be a case of consideration.

Here is the first substantial mentioning of beef and the first time one of the functions connected with roast beef, "carving," appears. After this the references to beef disappear for the rest of the still life.

In the next long still life, MUTTON, we see no mention of mutton until the very last passage.

A meal in mutton, mutton, why is lamb cheaper, it is cheaper because so little is more. Lecture, lecture and repeat instruction. (483)

After the food fragments begin to get smaller, we become more and more aware of distortions in the functions of individual words. In CUPS we see the following sentence: "Why is a cup a stir and a behave." (489) A cup can be stirred, but can it be a "stir?" And yet how can we argue with the logic of the juxtaposition, since stirring is something we associate with cups? The verb "behave" follows the article "a," a position in which we would ordinarily find another form of that word, "behavior." Miss Stein is still using language plastically.

The later still lifes of "Food" become, like those of "Objects," shorter and terser. Here is POTATOES: "Real potatoes cut in between." (490) A suggestion of French fried potatoes?

In the case of CELERY the description seems even more descriptive than suggestive: "Celery tastes tastes where in curled lashes and little bits and mostly in remains." (491) The iconicity here is surprising in comparison with what we have become accustomed to in the rest of

Tender Buttons. The "curled lashes" are the strings one peels away from celery in cleaning it. The "little bits" are perhaps the slices into which the celery is cut. The "remains" are probably the leaves at the end of the stalk that one throws away. In her treatment of the language Gertrude Stein tries to pretend that it did not exist before she began to write. But she does not pretend that there is not a world outside of her. It is very much there and it relates to what she is writing. But she forces the reader to recreate this external world for himself. She does not want to tell him what to see.

Nevertheless, she does attempt to use words in ways that they have never been used before. As *Tender Buttons* continues, the uses of words become even more wrenched out of their usual contexts. Here is a passage from EATING:

> Is it so a noise to be is it a least remain to rest, is it a so old say to be is it a leading are been. (494)

The verb "remain" appears in the function of a noun modified by an article and an adjective. Gertrude Stein is ignoring traditional morphology here (We would ordinarily add the ending *der* to "remain.") and in the next construction "a so old say," where we would normally add *ing* to "say." Also, the construction "a so old" would normally be written "such an old." The final construction is the most distorted of all. "Leading are been," because it is preceded by the article "a," must function in the sentence as a substantive, even though it is composed of three verb forms: the present participle, the simple present, and the past participle. In addition, neither the number or the tense of the verbs agree. "Are" should be in the past tense to agree with "been." However, it should be in the singular "is" form to agree with leading, which is rendered singular by being preceded by the article "a." All of the traditional functions of words and grammar mean nothing once language is used as a plastic material rather than as a communicative symbol.

The final section is entitled "Rooms," and, unlike the previous two parts of *Tender Buttons,* it is not divided into small subdivisions by a series of titles in capital letters. It is twelve pages of ostensibly unrelated paragraphs. However, other than these minor and obvious technical differences there is little to distinguish the writing in "Rooms" from that of either "Objects" or "Food." The individual paragraphs are constructed much the same as the previous still lifes, with just as much variety in their patterns as we saw before.

It is ironic that before *Tender Buttons,* and especially before this section on "Rooms," Miss Stein progressively excised in each succeeding book the use of setting, until at last in the portraits we have only a description of the character in no setting or social context whatever. And now in the final section of *Tender Buttons* we see a complete reversal of the previous trend in the abolition of people altogether, and a total emphasis, at least insofar as subject matter, on the physical surroundings. Of course, one direction is ultimately just as abstract as the other.

The connections in "Rooms" are made in much the same way that they were throughout the earlier parts of "Objects" and "Food." Between passages of seeming irrelevance we come on references to different parts of a room or on different objects that could be contained in a room. This section opens with the sentence, "Act so that there is no use in a centre." (498) We must assume the "centre" referred to as the center of the room. The first sentence of the next paragraph repeats this word and probably describes a curtain: "A whole centre and a border make hanging a way of dressing." And the last sentence of the same paragraph brings in another aspect of a room: "There was no rental."

Other references continue to build the picture of the room. "Any force which is bestowed on a floor shows rubbing." (499) And this piece of alliteration: "A little lingering lion and a Chinese chair . . ." There is even a picture of the author herself at work in her little room in her apartment on the rue de Fleurus: "The author of all that is in there behind the door and that is entering in the morning." There are continual references to "drawers," "doors," "floors," "table," "glasses," "table linen," "six little spoons," "windows," "mirrors," "beds," "springs," and many similar objects.

The same kinds of poetic devices as before are used in "Rooms." We have already seen an example of alliteration. There is also much use of rhyme, provided here by the repetition of *er* endings:

> A cape is a cover, a cape is not a cover in summer, a cape is a cover and the regulation is that there is no such weather. A cape is not always a cover, a cape is not a cover when there is another . . . (502)

Here is a full-scale poem in prose, with rhymes and a fairly strong rhythm:

> A religion, almost a religion, any religion, a quintal in religion, a relying and a surface and service in indecision and a creature and a question and a syllable in answer and more

counting and no quarrel and a single scientific statement and
no darkness and no question and an earned administration
and a single set of sister and an outline and no blisters.
(505)

Occasional examples of striking metaphors still occur,
as in "elastic tumbler," although there is no example of
the dislocation of words from their traditional functions
as we saw in "Objects" and "Food." There are no real
stylistic innovations that are original with "Rooms." Miss
Stein merely maintains here the same general level of
abstractionism that she has already established.

Before we leave *Tender Buttons,* however, there is one
more problem to explore. What are the sources of the
"seemingly irrelevant" passages that appear among the
realistic suggestions referring to the supposed subject of
the writing? It seems to me that Gertrude Stein allows
"irrelevancies" to creep into her writing in much the
same way that a number of modern artists have brought
things into their works that have no conceivable relation
to what they are doing. I refer here to the admission of
accident, matters of purely personal interest, or stray
thoughts that may have wandered into the mind at the
moment. Richard Ellmann tells an anecdote along these
lines in his biography of James Joyce. This incident occurred during the writing of *Finnegans Wake* when
Samuel Beckett was Joyce's amanuensis:

Once or twice he dictated a bit of *Finnegans Wake* to Beckett,
though dictation did not work very well for him; in the middle
of one such session there was a knock at the door which Beckett
didn't hear. Joyce said, 'Come in,' and Beckett wrote it down.
Afterwards he read back what he had written and Joyce said
'What's that "Come in"?' 'Yes, you said that,' said Beckett. Joyce

thought for a moment, then said, 'Let it stand.' He was quite willing to accept coincidence as his collaborator. Beckett was fascinated and thwarted by Joyce's singular method.[11]

Thornton Wilder has similar information to give about Gertrude Stein's methods of composition.

She introduces what I like to call "the irruption of the daily life." If her two dogs are playing at her feet while she is writing she puts them into the text. She may suddenly introduce some phrases she has just heard over the garden wall. This resembles a practice that her friends the Post-impressionist painters occasionally resorted to. They pasted a subway ticket to the surface of their painting. The reality of a work of art is one reality; the reality of a "thing" is another reality; the juxtaposition of the two kinds of reality gives a bracing shock. It also insults the reader; but the reader is not present, nor even imagined. It refreshes in the writer the sense that the writer is all alone, alone with his thoughts and his struggle and even with his relation to the outside world that lies about him.[12]

A number of Wilder's statements seem relevant to the method of *Tender Buttons*. First of all, Gertrude Stein is willing to introduce anything into the context of her writing. At one point, as we noted, in "Rooms" she introduces herself behind the door, presumably writing. Also, Wilder's statement that "the juxtaposition of the two kinds of reality gives a bracing shock" seems to me to be the main rationale for what Gertrude Stein is doing in *Tender Buttons*. It is the startling juxtaposition, the strange metaphor, the emergence of reality occasionally from the midst of unintelligibility, the exotic uses of words, the syntactic discontinuities that give to *Tender Buttons* whatever it has that is striking and original.

[11] *James Joyce* (New York, 1959), p. 662.
[12] "Introduction," *Four in America* (New Haven, 1947), p. xv.

Gertrude Stein says as much herself near the end of *Tender Buttons:*

> Surprise, the only surprise has no occasion. It is an ingredient and the section the whole section is one season. (509)

In addition to the elements of surprise and the admission of external reality into the created object, Miss Stein was constantly including in her writing what James and Bergson call "the immediate data of consciousness."[13] Her immediate perceptions, her thoughts about certain nagging problems, her questions about certain objects or themes that appear in her writing, the associations that a word or sound might set off in her conscious mind, all of these are for Gertrude Stein legitimate materials for her writing. Her method of composition seems to go something like this. She focuses directly on a particular subject for as long as it may stick in her mind. Then she may depart from the subject to follow an association or report something that has entered her consciousness. The subject at hand returns again and again, but the importance of this whole retrospective process is to express the continuous present on-going of her consciousness. This is, after all, the only pure knowledge according to her theory. If data other than that relating directly to the supposed subject intrude into her consciousness, then they must be recorded as a manifestation of Gertrude Stein's process of thought. This would explain the peculiar structure of the writing known as *Tender Buttons,* its continual digressions and sudden intrusions of reality.

This is the method and result to which all the previous

[13] Bergson wrote an entire book on the subject in *Time and Free Will,* first published in French in 1889.

writings of Gertrude Stein have led. The path of abstractionism, as we have seen, was a slow and careful development, on which each piece of writing served as a new obstacle to be overcome, until the genuine step into the abstract style was possible. It is the prolific effort of a number of years that finally leads to the creation of the first piece of writing ever to create completely its own world and its own set of conventions by which it demands to be approached and judged. In this sense, Gertrude Stein is a profoundly original writer, and we have watched her move through progressive stages to this totally unique result.

However, uniqueness is not a necessary measure of aesthetic value. Therefore, the reader who decides ultimately that the writings of Gertrude Stein do not satisfy his criteria of what great literature should be is perhaps entitled to put most of them down as experiments that fail to please. But no serious student of contemporary literature should allow himself to dismiss their author as an eccentric who should be "defined out of existence as an artist."[14] It is incumbent on all of us to at least understand what Gertrude Stein was doing, for in her writings she went a long way toward defining the limits of language. Young writers, especially, can learn as much from her in this direction as they can from the more popular James Joyce.

It is fruitless to lament the existence of Gertrude Stein or to ridicule her as both a person and writer. Whatever place posterity assigns her in the literary chain of being, one cannot escape the fact of the very large shelf of

[14] Ben Reid, *Art by Subtraction: A Dissenting Opinion of Gertrude Stein* (Norman, Okla., 1958), p. 170.

books she produced and which still have the power to excite such extremes of rapture and indignation. Miss Stein is an historical fact and we cannot wish her away. As John Malcolm Brinnin has said,

> If Gertrude Stein had never lived, sooner or later works very much like those she produced would have been written by someone else. Once a particular set of conditions was present, her arrival was inevitable—like an event in chemistry.[15]

If Gertrude Stein was an inevitability for the twentieth century, then as products of the same age we can probably learn much about ourselves in her enigmatic works. The supposed irrationality of her writing may be no more than a reflection of the irrationality of our world. To understand the enigma of Gertrude Stein, however, we must first try to determine what there is in her writing, free from all the cant surrounding her personality. The present study, it is hoped, is a first step in this attempt.

[15] *The Third Rose: Gertrude Stein and Her World* (Boston, 1959), p. xiv.

Appendix

A. GERTRUDE STEIN IN THE PSYCHOLOGY LABORATORY

READERS OF *The Autobiography of Alice B. Toklas* know that Gertrude Stein worked in experimental psychology under William James. She was at the time a Radcliffe undergraduate, and her previous mentor in psychology, Hugo Münsterberg, had found her "the model of what a young scholar should be."[1] With another young student, Leon Solomons, the precocious Miss Stein worked on such projects as "The Place of Repetition in Memory," "Fluctuations of the Attention," and "The Saturation of Colors," including herself among the subjects.[2] In September 1896, they published some results of their experiments as "Normal Motor Automatism," in the *Psychological Review*.[3] Two years later Gertrude Stein alone wrote another article based on the same experiments.[4] These first publications prefigure

[1] John Malcolm Brinnin, *The Third Rose: Gertrude Stein and Her World* (Boston, 1959), p. 29.
[2] *Ibid.*
[3] III (1896), 492-512. Solomons died in 1900 from an infection contracted in the laboratory.
[4] "Cultivated Motor Automatism," *Psychological Review*, V (1898), 295-306.

some of the controlling ideas in her earliest fiction, and they are worth examining for the light they can shed on *Things as They Are, Three Lives, The Making of Americans,* and *Tender Buttons.*

Gertrude Stein and Leon Solomons were mainly interested in testing the limits of their subjects' attention. They asked them to write repeatedly the same letter while reading a story aloud. In another experiment, the subject read a story aloud while attempting to record words that Miss Stein or Mr. Solomons read to him. In another, the subject tried to read aloud a dull story while listening to an interesting one. The experimenters wanted to discover the limits of conscious attention, by seeing how long a person could concentrate before fatigue would allow his unconscious reactions to disturb his attentiveness.

What they discovered was that the average person's attention began to waver almost immediately. Especially when asked to write the same letter repeatedly, the subjects began involuntarily to write words from the story. Even when conscious of repeating the same involuntary action, they were still unable to prevent it. Moreover, the subject wrote with seemingly no break in his attention to what was being read. This indicated that in most instances unconscious reactions could not be completely overridden by conscious attention. One exception to the rule, however, was Gertrude Stein herself, who, as she later directs Alice B. Toklas to say, "never had subconscious reactions, nor was she a successful subject for automatic writing."[5]

As it turned out, the most notorious experiment was

[5] *The Autobiography of Alice B. Toklas,* p. 79.

ultimately "automatic writing." A planchette with a pencil was hung from the ceiling, and the subject was instructed to hold the pencil over a piece of paper while one of the experimenters read a story to him. If the subject began to write even while concentrating on the story, the assumption would be that his hand was being unconsciously directed. This particular experiment met with only moderate success, many of the subjects producing nothing but scribbles and gibberish. However, enough students responded "automatically" to allow Miss Stein and Mr. Solomons to make the following generalization: automatic writing reveals *"a marked tendency to repetition* [their italics]—A phrase would seem to get into the head and keep repeating itself at every opportunity, and hang over from day to day even."[6] An example they used, " 'When he could not be the longest and thus to be, and thus to be, the strongest,' "[7] reads suspiciously like a line from Gertrude Stein's later writings.

In 1934 the Harvard behaviorist, B. F. Skinner, rediscovered this early article and wrote about it in the *Atlantic Monthly*. In "Normal Motor Automatism," Professor Skinner claimed to have found the key to the ambiguities of *Tender Buttons,* in lines such as the one in the previous paragraph: the writings in *Tender Buttons* are examples of automatic writing. However, they are less the writings of a second or unconscious personality than of Gertrude Stein's arm.

. . . although it is quite plausible that the work is due to a second personality successfully split off from Miss Stein's con-

[6] "Normal Motor Automatism," 506.
[7] *Ibid.*

scious self, it is a very flimsy sort of personality indeed. It is intellectually unopinionated, is emotionally cold, and has no past. It is unread and unlearned beyond grammar school. It is as easily influenced as a child; a heard word may force itself into whatever sentence may be under construction at the moment, or it may break the sentence up altogether and irremediably. Its literary materials are the sensory things nearest at hand—objects, sounds, tastes, smells, and so on.[8]

Although written in a debunking spirit, Professor Skinner's remarks are a more than adequate description of some of the major characteristics of Gertrude Stein's writing. What he has described is Miss Stein's conception of the "human mind," which she contrasts to "human nature." To Miss Stein, human nature is that part of man's consciousness that makes relationships among objects, that has memory, that self-consciously refers back to its own identity, that has emotions, that is burdened with knowledge outside its immediate perceptions. The human mind has no emotions, memory, identity, or past. It is simply that part of the human consciousness that does nothing but perceive whatever data is immediately available to the senses. The process of writing transfers the knowledge of the human mind to paper as quickly as it is perceived. It has nothing to do with any past knowledge because "the human mind knows what it knows and knowing what it knows it has nothing to do with seeing what it remembers. . . ."[9]

Though Professor Skinner's description of the consciousness that wrote *Tender Buttons* may be accurate,

[8] "Has Gertrude Stein a Secret?" *Atlantic,* CLIII (January 1934), 53.
[9] Gertrude Stein, *The Geographical History of America* (New York, 1936), p. 27. This work contains Miss Stein's fullest discussion of "human nature" and "human mind."

his accusation that Miss Stein wrote automatically is not. Quite aware of the characteristics of "automatic writing," Gertrude Stein developed some of its surface attributes into a conscious aesthetic. Only by writing consciously could Gertrude Stein consistently maintain a style that excluded so many elements of "human nature." The surrealists used automatic writing to delve into the fantasies of the unconscious. But the unconscious, as any reader of Freud knows, has everything to do with the past, with identity, and with emotions, all of which Gertrude Stein consciously attempts to outlaw from her writing. To contend that she sat in her studio waiting for impulses to direct her hand over the page, and in this way managed to produce forty books or more, stretches credibility. If the consciousness that created *Tender Buttons* strikes Professor Skinner as "unread and unlearned beyond grammar school," perhaps Laura Riding had answered that contention already:

> Gertrude Stein, by combining the functions of critic and poet and taking everything around her very literally and many things for granted which others have not been naive enough to take so, has done what everyone else has been ashamed to do. No one but she has been willing to be as ordinary, as simple, as primitive, as stupid, as barbaric as successful barbarism demands.[10]

We can learn even more of relevance to Miss Stein's creative writings from her second article. Leon Solomons wrote most of the first article himself, although Gertrude Stein may have had a hand in the revisions. Indeed, she disagreed with many of the conclusions favorable to automatic writing. In the article she wrote under her

[10] "The New Barbarian and Gertrude Stein," *transition*, I (June 1927), 157.

own name in 1898, she gave more attention to things that particularly interested her. She described this many years later:

> Then as I say I became more interested in psychology, and one of the things I did was testing reactions of the average college student in a state of normal activity and in the state of fatigue induced by their examinations. I was supposed to be interested in their reactions but soon I found that I was not but instead that I was enormously interested in the types of their characters that is what I even then thought of as the bottom nature of them, and when in May 1898 I wrote my half of the report of these experiments I expressed these results as follows:
> In these descriptions it will be readily observed that habits of attention are reflexes of the complete character of the individual.[11]

The key word in this paragraph is "type." Moreover, it is not a word Gertrude Stein decided to use forty years later to discuss the rationale behind her own writing, but one that appears over and over in the 1898 article. Gertrude Stein asks in the beginning of her article how the different "types of character" react to automatic writing.[12] She was mainly interested in the people involved in her experiments and not the data they provided; not their reactions to what they were doing but how they seemed to her to manifest themselves as prototypes. This prefigures her early fictional method in which the action of the individual is less important than how his actions follow from a typologically determined personality.

The experiments had derived their subjects primarily

---

[11] "The Gradual Making of The Making of Americans," *Lectures in America* (Boston, 1957), pp. 137-38.
[12] "Cultivated Motor Automatism," 295.

from Radcliffe and Harvard students, some of whom Miss Stein describes as follows:

A large number of my subjects were New Englanders, and the habit of self-repression, the intense self-consciousness, the morbid fear of "letting one's self go," that is so prominent an element in the New England character, was a constant stumbling-block.[13]

The article is full of her personal and undocumented (indeed, undocumentable) observations, and it would almost certainly not be accepted by a scientific journal today; but we can be thankful for the relaxed standards of a young science, for the article affords valuable evidence of Miss Stein's continuing notions of the innate personality of different types and the characteristics that make up the "bottom natures" of people. Five years later, in *Things as They Are,* Miss Stein used almost the exact attributes ascribed above to her New England type in the characterization of Sophie Neathe. Once could probably take the typological descriptions from this article and find corresponding fictional characters in Miss Stein's writing. However, that kind of detective work seems less important than discovering in the article the earliest published evidence of Miss Stein's theory of psychological types.

Gertrude Stein divided her subjects into a number of categories:

Type I. This consists mostly of girls who are found naturally in literature courses and men who are going in for law. The type is nervous, high strung, very imaginative, has the capacity to be easily roused and intensely interested. Their attention is strongly and easily held by something that inter-

[13] *Ibid.,* 299.

ests them, even to the extent quite commonly expressed of being oblivious to everything else. But, on the other hand, they find it hard to concentrate on anything that does not catch the attention and hold the interest.[14]

The personal judgments and generalizations of this passage would make a contemporary psychologist smile; but Gertrude Stein is only warming up.

Type II is very different from Type I, is more varied, and gives more interesting results. In general, the individuals, often blonde and pale, are distinctly phlegmatic. If emotional, decidedly of a weakish sentimental order. They may be either large, healthy, rather heavy and lacking in vigor, or they may be what we call anaemic and phlegmatic. Their power of concentrated attention is very small. They describe themselves as never being held by their work; they say that their minds wander easily; that they work on after they are tired and just keep pegging away.[15]

These are the kinds of assumptions Gertrude Stein was willing to make; but I do not propose to judge her as a scientist. Had she been a good scientist rather than one merely scientifically inclined, she might never have turned to writing fiction.

What we can learn from this article is that five years before Miss Stein began to write her first fictional work her conception of personality was already formed around the notion of the controlling type. In her long descriptions she lists not only physical characteristics, but mental, emotional, and other behavioral traits. She subsumed all facets of the individual as a behavioral organism under the characteristics of the type.

This becomes apparent in writings such as *Three*

[14] *Ibid.*, 297.
[15] *Ibid.*, 297-98.

Lives and *The Making of Americans,* in which the characters function almost solely as demonstrations of a proposition made by the author about a personality type. The type arises from racial, national, or parental heritage, and it is something no one can escape. Miss Stein says in the opening lines of *The Making of Americans,* "It is hard living down the tempers we are born with."[16] Personality arises directly from the type into which we are born, and all the characteristics of the individual are determined thereby. These notions are expressed quite clearly in "Cultivated Motor Automatism," and we must turn to it to understand the origins of Miss Stein's static fictional portraits.

Gertrude Stein's deterministic theories of personality had, if not their beginnings, then certanly a great part of their development in William James' laboratory. Her concepts of consciousness and the deterministic type, the two pillars of her theory of personality, were developed long before she began to publish fictional constructs of her ideas.

B. GERTRUDE STEIN AND WILLIAM JAMES

"The important person in Gertrude Stein's Radcliffe life was William James." Thus speaks Alice B. Toklas in her *Autobiography.* "William James delighted her. His personality and his teaching and his way of amusing himself with himself and his students all pleased her."[1] The ties of Gertrude Stein and William James were more

[16] *The Making of Americans* (Paris, 1925), p. 3.
[1] Gertrude Stein, *The Autobiography of Alice B. Toklas* (New York, 1933), p. 78.

than those of student and mentor; they transcended the roles and became those of the closest mutual friendship and regard lasting until the death of James. A number of apocryphal stories, more or less believable, have grown around the student-teacher relationship. However, Gertrude Stein in a student theme has stated her esteem better than anyone else:

Is life worth living? Yes, a thousand times yes when the world still holds such spirits as Professor James. He is truly a man among men; a scientist of force and originality embodying all that is strongest and worthiest in the scientific spirit; a metaphysician skilled in abstract thought, clear and vigorous and yet too great to worship logic as his God, and narrow himself to a belief merely in the reason of man.

A man he is who has lived sympathetically not alone all thought but all life. He stands firmly, nobly for the dignity of man. His faith is not that of a cringing coward before an all-powerful master, but of a strong man willing to fight, to suffer and endure. He has not accepted faith because it is easy and pleasing. He has thought and lived many years and at last says with a voice of authority, if life does not mean this, I don't know what it means.

What can one say more? His is a strong sane noble personality reacting truly on all experience that life has given him. He is a man take him for all in all.[2]

Gertrude Stein's admiration was obviously profound, and she did not renounce this early affection when she came to write about it thirty-five years later, at a time that she denied the obvious influence of Henry James.

Affection between two individuals does not mean that one will necessarily influence the other, but this evidence of Gertrude Stein's regard for William James should at least demonstrate the potentially open frame

[2] Rosalind S. Miller, *Gertrude Stein: Form and Intelligibility* (New York, 1949), pp. 146-7.

of mind with which she received James' ideas. Others have already discussed ways in which the ideas of both Stein and James seem to correspond significantly;[3] it is those areas in which William James, both as psychologist and philosopher, can illuminate the abstract style of Gertrude Stein that I now wish to explore.

William James' earliest conception of consciousness, as expounded in *The Principles of Psychology,* was of an entity containing "a teeming multiplicity of objects and relations . . ."; and further, "what we call simple sensations are results of discriminative attention, pushed often to a very high degree."[4] It was during the years immediately following publication of his major book that Gertrude Stein worked under James in the Harvard psychology laboratory. Assuming the Jamesian conception of consciousness as an entity expressing itself most strongly in habits and powers of attention, she and Leon Solomons conducted a series of experiments exploring their subjects' attributes of attention. We have seen how Miss Stein's somewhat rigid concept of consciousness arose out of these experiments. She came to feel that people can be differentiated into types according to how their consciousness manifests itself through their patterns of attention. This concept of the type arising out of the entity of consciousness and controlling the habits of attention dominates Miss Stein's character portrayals until after *The Making of Americans.*

By the time James came to write *Essays in Radical*

[3] Ronald Bartlett Levinson, "Gertrude Stein, William James and Grammar," *Am. Journal of Psych.,* LIV (Jan. 1941); Allegra Stewart, "Quality of Gertrude Stein's Creativity," *Am. Lit.,* XXVIII (Jan. 1957), 488-506; Donald Sutherland, "The Elements," *Gertrude Stein: A Biography of Her Work* (New Haven, 1951), pp. 1-21.

[4] (New York, 1890), v. 1, p. 224.

Empiricism, however, he had long since begun to doubt his intellectualist formulation of the entity of consciousness.

> For twenty years past I have mistrusted "consciousness" as an entity; for seven or eight years past I have suggested its non-existence to my students, and tried to give them its pragmatic equivalent in realities of experience. It seems to me that the hour is ripe for it to be openly and universally discarded.

> Let me then immediately explain that I mean only to deny that the word stands for an entity, but to insist most emphatically that it does stand for a function.[5]

This conception of consciousness as a function rather than an entity had at least been adumbrated in *Principles of Psychology* in James' chapter on the "Stream of Thought."

> Consciousness, then, does not appear to itself chopped up in bits. Such words as 'chain' or 'train' do not describe it fitly as it presents itself in the first instance. It is nothing jointed; it flows. A 'river' or a 'stream' are the metaphors by which it is most naturally described. *In talking of it hereafter, let us call it the stream of thought, of consciousness, or of subjective life.*[6] (Italics James')

Here we see the stream of thought contained within the entity of consciousness. Later, however, consciousness will become the stream itself. Now, there is a difference between thought and consciousness, as Donald Sutherland has pointed out.[7] Consciousness is the flow of ideas, thoughts, sensations, and perceptions through the mind. But thought implies something deliberately chosen, something on which attention is focused. James' prefer-

[5] (New York, 1912), p. 3.
[6] v. I, p. 239.
[7] Sutherland, *op. cit.,* p. 4.

ence for "thought" rather than "consciousness" in this early book is consistent with his emphasis on habits of attention as the prime manifestation of consciousness.

In Gertrude Stein's earliest writings she maintains James' original conceptions. Her characters are not only types, but they are also defined mainly by the kind of thought that inhabits their consciousness—thoughts almost never irrelevant to a demonstration of their "bottom natures." We never see any of the stray bits of irrelevance that travel through the average consciousness. Miss Stein presents her characters only when they are focusing their attention on something, and we never see them during their inattentive moments. As we saw in the discussion of her experiments, she thought herself incapable of inattentiveness. If this is so, then her presentation of fictional characters may reflect her concept of her own consciousness.

Miss Stein's rigid concept of consciousness softens around the time that James' does. At the end of *The Making of Americans* we are aware of the beginnings of the gradual loosening of "attention" on the part of the narrator, who begins to take over completely as the central consciousness of her work. In *A Long Gay Book* this central consciousness has begun to allow his attention to relax to the point of admitting thoughts totally unrelated to the central focus of the subject matter. In the "portraits" and finally in *Tender Buttons* Miss Stein gives the stream of consciousness free rein to make its own associations on the basis of sounds, rhythms, and syntactical patterns. Attention returns again and again to put the consciousness back on the subject of the discourse, only to have it wander off as soon as it makes an association of its own.

In this way the stream of consciousness proceeds, including both thought and the other elements of the stream that have heretofore been submerged. This is not to imply that Miss Stein's consciousness was lacking in attention; rather, she allowed the central consciousness of her writings to let its attention waver and give expression to the continuous stream of itself.

Gertrude Stein began to feel more and more that only the present contents of her mind, the "immediate data of her consciousness," were of genuine creative importance. It was not in well-formulated thoughts depending on memory for both their content and structure that one could express his own bottom nature, but in recording the continual ongoing of the stream of his own personality. Miss Stein wanted to express thoughts that are pre-verbal, or have at least not been formalized into an organized syntactical structure. James had discussed this problem in connection with the stream of thought:

> The object of every thought, then, is neither more nor less than all that the thought thinks, exactly as the thought thinks it, however complicated the matter, and however symbolic the manner of the thinking may be. It is needless to say that memory can seldom accurately reproduce such an object, when once it has passed from before the mind. It either makes too little or too much of it. Its best plan is to repeat the verbal sentence, if there was one, in which the object was expressed. But for inarticulate thoughts there is not even this resource, and introspection must confess that the task exceeds her powers. The mass of our thinking vanishes forever, beyond hope of recovery, and psychology only gathers up a few of the crumbs that fall from the feast.[8]

Gertrude Stein wanted to give up all reliance on intro-

[8] *The Principles of Psychology*, v. 1, p. 276.

spection and try the seemingly impossible task of capturing the inarticulate stream of her own consciousness. This, it seems to me, is the key to her creative methods in such writings as the "portraits" and *Tender Buttons.* Gertrude Stein was thoroughly familiar with the writings of William James and could hardly have avoided reading statements such as the above. Whether the close correspondence of some of their ideas is due to direct influence is a matter fruitless to determine, but the similarities seem hardly to be accidental.

Other statements by James about linguistic conventions are relevant to techniques in the later writings of Miss Stein's early period.

> How comes it about that a man reading something aloud for the first time is able immediately to emphasize all his words aright, unless from the very first he have a sense of at least the form of the sentence yet to come, which sense is fused with his consciousness of the present word, and modifies its emphasis in his mind so as to make him give it the proper accent as he utters it? Emphasis of this kind is almost altogether a matter of grammatical construction. If we read "no more" we expect presently to come upon a "than"; if we read "however" at the outset of a sentence it is a "yet", a "still", or a "nevertheless", that we expect. A noun in a certain position demands a verb in a certain mood and number, in another position it expects a relative pronoun. Adjectives call for nouns, verbs for adverbs, etc., etc.[9]

The conventions that William James describes here are the very ones Miss Stein violates in her syntactically discontinous style. We have seen how Miss Stein violates every kind of expectancy James has listed. It is almost as though she wanted to prove that the whole system of

[9] *Ibid.,* p. 263.

verbal communication is a set of formalized habits to
which no writer is beholden. Since the contemporary
artist creates his own conventions, then that writer who
had escaped from his dependence on the past would report the contents of his consciousness in the form that
they came to his mind and not reform them by any conventions—linguistic or otherwise—that depend on memory or tradition.

One of Gertrude Stein's almost seductive techniques
presents the reader with a series of sentences of traditional syntax, modifies them slowly with a series of discontinuities, and then continues the modification until
the reader suddenly discovers that the past few sentences he has read make no sense whatsoever. The
reader realizes that his mind has managed to adapt all of
the sentences to something resembling traditional meanings because his psychological set is almost unwilling to
accept any violations of its expectancies. James had discussed this characteristic of the human mind many years
before Gertrude Stein was to challenge it in her writing.

> So delicate and incessant is this recognition by the mind of
> the mere fitness of words to be mentioned together that the
> slightest misreading, such as "casualty" for 'causality,' or "per-
> petual" for "perceptual," will be corrected by a listener whose
> attention is so relaxed that he gets no idea of the *meaning* of the
> sentence at all.
> Conversely, if words do belong to the same vocabulary, and
> if the grammatical structure is correct, sentences with abso-
> lutely no meaning may be uttered in good faith and pass
> unchallenged.[10]

[10] *Ibid.*, p. 263.

James has outlined quite neatly before the fact why most readers find Gertrude Stein's abstract writings so disruptive to their sensibilities. They discover that a lifetime development of reading, speaking, and writing habits go for naught. If all original art is disorientative to minds versed in traditional forms, then Gertrude Stein's writings are so totally disruptive that they unfortunately do almost nothing but arouse frustration, anger, and ultimately ridicule.

Selected Bibliography

This bibliography includes only those items definitely of aid on the specific subject of the book. I have listed the works in separate categories to make more clear the specific ways various entries were useful.

BIBLIOGRAPHIES OF WRITINGS OF AND ON GERTRUDE STEIN

Firmage, George James. *A Check-list of the Published Writings of Gertrude Stein*. Amherst, Mass.: U. of Mass. Press, 1954.

Haas, Robert Bartlett and Donald Clifford Gallup. *A Catalogue of the Published and Unpublished Writings of Gertrude Stein*. New Haven: Yale U. Press, 1941.

Sawyer, Julian. *Gertrude Stein. A Bibliography*. New York: Arrow Editions, 1941.

————. "Gertrude Stein (1874-   ): A Checklist Comprising Critical and Miscellaneous Writings about Her Work, Life and Personality from 1913-1942,"

Bul. Bibl., XVII (Jan.-Apr. 1943), 211-12; XVIII (May-Aug. 1943), 11-13.

————. "Gertrude Stein: A Bibliography, 1941-1948," *Bul. Bibl.,* XIX (May-Aug., Sept.-Dec. 1948), 152-56, 183-87.

Stein, Gertrude. "Bibliography," *transition,* III (Feb. 1929), 47-55.

GERTRUDE STEIN'S WRITINGS

"American Language and Literature," unpub. ms. in Yale U. Lib.

The Autobiography of Alice B. Toklas. New York: Random House, 1933.

"Cultivated Motor Automatism: A Study of Character in Its Relation to Attention," *Psych. Rev.,* V (May 1898), 295-306.

Everybody's Autobiography. New York: Random House, 1937.

Four in America, introd. Thornton Wilder. New Haven: Yale U. Press, 1947.

The Geographical History of America. New York: Random House, 1936.

Geography and Plays. Boston: Four Seas Press, 1922.

How to Write. Paris: Plain Edition, 1931.

Lectures in America. Boston: Beacon Press, 1957.

Letter to Alfred Stieglitz, May 6, 1921, unpub. TLS, Yale U. Library.

The Making of Americans. Paris: Contact Editions, 1925.

The Making of Americans, abridged version. New York: Harcourt, Brace, 1934.

Matisse Picasso and Gertrude Stein: with two shorter stories. Paris: Plain Edition, 1932.

Narration. Chicago: U. of Chicago Press, 1935.

"Normal Motor Automatism," with Leon Solomons, *Psych. Rev.,* III (1896), 492-512.

Picasso. London: B. T. Batsford, 1948.

Portraits and Prayers. New York: Random House, 1934.

Selected Writings of Gertrude Stein, ed. and introd. Carl Van Vechten. New York: Modern Library, 1962.

Things as They Are. Pawlet, Vt.: Banyan Press, 1950.

Three Lives. New York: Modern Library, 1936.

Two: Gertrude Stein and Her Brother, and Other Early Portraits. New Haven: Yale U. Press, 1951.

Useful Knowledge. New York, 1928.

What Are Masterpieces, introd. Robert Bartlett Haas. Los Angeles: The Conference Press, 1940.

BOOKS AND ARTICLES ON GERTRUDE STEIN, OR IN WHICH COMMENTARY ON GERTRUDE STEIN APPEARS

Aldington, Richard. "The Disciples of Gertrude Stein," *Poetry,* XVII (Oct. 1920), 35-40.

Anonymous. "Three Lives," *Nation,* XC (Jan. 20, 1910), 65.

Baldanza, Frank. "Faulkner and Stein: A Study in Stylistic Intransigence," *Georgia Rev.,* XIII (Fall 1959), 274-286.

Bridgman, Richard. "Melanctha," *Am. Lit.,* XXXIII (Nov. 1961), 350-9.

Brinnin, John Malcolm. *The Third Rose: Gertrude Stein and Her World.* Boston: Little, Brown, 1959.

Burke, Kenneth. "Engineering with Words," *Dial,* LXXIV (April 1923), 408-12.

Cargill, Oscar. *Intellectual America, Ideas on the March.* New York: MacMillan, 1941

Church, Ralph. "A Note on the Writing of Gertrude Stein," *transition,* XIV (June 1927), 184-8.

Corke, Hilary. "Reflections on a Great Stone Face: The Achievement of Gertrude Stein," *Kenyon Rev.,* XXIII (Summer 1961), 367-89.

Dupee, F. W. "Gertrude Stein," *Commentary,* XXXIII (June 1962), 519-23.

Eagelson, Harvey. "Gertrude Stein: Method in Madness," *Sewanee Rev.,* XLIV (Apr.-June 1936), 164-77.

Evans, Oliver. "Gertrude Stein as Humorist," *Prairie Schooner,* XXI (Spring 1947), 97-102.

————. "The Americanism of Gertrude Stein," *Prairie Schooner,* XXII (Spring 1948), 70-74.

Gallup, Donald C. "A Book is a Book is a Book: A History of the Writing and Publication of Gertrude Stein's *Three Lives,*" *New Colophon,* I (Jan. 1948), 67-80.

————. "The Gertrude Stein Collection," *Yale U. Lib. Gazette,* XXII (Oct. 1947), 22-32.

————. "The Making of *The Making of Americans,*" *New Colophon,* III (1950), 54-74.

Garvin, H. R. "Gertrude Stein: A Study of Her Theory and Practice," unpub. doc. diss. Michigan, 1950.

Gass, William H. "Gertrude Stein: Her Escape from Protective Language," *Accent,* XVIII (Autumn 1958), 233-244.

Haines, George IV. "Forms of Imaginative Prose: 1900-1940," *Southern Rev.*, VII (Spring 1942), 755-75.

————. "Gertrude Stein and Composition," *Sewanee Rev.*, LVII (Summer 1949), 411-24.

Hoffman, Frederick J. *Gertrude Stein.* U. of Minnesota Pamphlets, No. 10. Minneapolis, 1961.

Hoffman, Michael J. "Gertrude Stein in the Psychology Laboratory," *Am. Quarterly*, XVII (Spring 1965), 127-32.

Lachman, Arthur. "Gertrude Stein as I Knew Her," unpub. ms. in Yale U. Library.

Lane, J. W. "The Craze for Craziness," *Cath. World*, CXLIV (Dec. 1936), 306-09.

Leach, Wilford. "Gertrude Stein and the Modern Theatre," unpub. doc. diss. Illinois, 1956.

Levinson, Ronald Bartlett. "Gertrude Stein, William James and Grammar," *Am. Journal of Psych.*, LIV (Jan. 1941), 124-8.

Lowe, Frederick W. "Gertrude's Web: A Study of Gertrude Stein's Literary Relationships," unpub. doc. diss. Columbia, 1957.

Mercier, Vivian. "In Joyce's Wake, a Booming Industry," *NYTBR*, LXVI (July 30, 1961), 5, 20-1.

Miller, Rosalind S. *Gertrude Stein: Form and Intelligibility.* New York: Exposition Press, 1949.

Pearson, Norman H. "The Gertrude Stein Collection," *Yale U. Lib. Gazette*, XVI (Jan. 1942), 45-7.

Porter, Katherine Anne. *The Days Before.* New York: Harcourt, Brace, 1952.

Reid, Ben. *Art by Subtraction: A Dissenting Opinion of Gertrude Stein.* Norman, Okla.: U. of Oklahoma Press, 1958.

Riding, Laura. "The New Barbarian and Gertrude Stein," *transition,* I (June 1927), 153-68.

Rogers, W. G. *When This You See Remember Me.* New York: Rinehart, 1948.

Saarinen, Aline B. "The Steins in Paris," *Am. Scholar,* XXVII (Autumn 1958), 437-48.

Skinner, B. F. "Has Gertrude Stein a Secret?" *Atlantic* CLIII (Jan. 1934), 50-7.

Sprigge, Elizabeth. *Gertrude Stein: Her Life and Work.* New York: Harper, 1957.

Stein, Leo. *Journey into the Self.* New York: Crown, 1950.

Stewart, Allegra. "Quality of Gertrude Stein's Creativity," *Am. Lit.,* XXVIII (Jan. 1957), 488-506.

Sutherland, Donald. *Gertrude Stein: A Biography of Her Work.* New Haven: Yale U. Press, 1951.

Wilcox, Wendell. "A Note on Stein and Abstraction," *Poetry,* LV (Feb. 1940), 254-57.

Wilson, Edmund. *Axel's Castle.* New York: Scribner's, 1931.

―――. *The Shores of Light: A Literary Chronicle of the Twenties and Thirties.* New York: Farrar, Straus & Cudahy, 1952.

WORKS USED PRIMARILY AS BACKGROUND MATERIAL: HISTORICAL, CRITICAL, AND METHODOLOGICAL

Apollinaire, Guillaume. *The Cubist Painters: Aesthetic Meditations,* trans. Lionel Abel. New York: Wittenborn, Schultz, 1949.

Bergson, Henri. *Creative Evolution,* trans. Arthur Mitchell. New York: Henry Holt, 1911.

———. *Introduction to Metaphysics,* trans. T. E. Hulme. New York: Putnam, 1912.

———. *Matter and Memory,* trans. Nancy Margaret Paul and W. Scott Palmer. Garden City, N.Y.: Doubleday Anchor, 1959.

———. *Time and Free Will,* trans. F. L. Pogson. New York: Harper Torchbooks, 1960.

Ellmann, Richard. *James Joyce.* New York: Oxford, 1959.

Flaubert, Gustave. *Three Tales,* trans. Arthur McDowall. Norfolk, Conn.: New Directions, 1947.

Frank, Joseph. "Spatial Form in Modern Literature," *Sewanee Rev.,* LIII (Sum. and Aut. 1945), 221-40, 433-56, 643-53.

Frye, Northrop. *Anatomy of Criticism.* Princeton: Princeton U. Press, 1957.

Gallup, Donald, ed. *The Flowers of Friendship: Letters Written to Gertrude Stein.* New York: Knopf, 1953.

Hoffman, Frederick J. *The Twenties: American Writing in the Postwar Decade.* New York: Viking, 1955.

Humphrey, Robert. *Stream of Consciousness in the Modern Novel.* Berkeley and Los Angeles: U. of California Press, 1954.

James, William. *Essays in Radical Empiricism.* New York: Longmans, Green, 1912.

———. *The Meaning of Truth: A Sequel to Pragmatism.* New York: Longmans, Green, 1909.

———. *A Pluralistic Universe.* New York: Longmans, Green, 1909.

———. *Pragmatism: A New Name for Some Old*

Ways of Thinking. New York: Longmans, Green, 1910.

————. *The Principles of Psychology,* 2 vols., New York: Henry Holt, 1890.

Kandinsky, Wassily. *Concerning the Spiritual in Art,* trans. Michael Sadleir. New York: Wittenborn, Schultz, 1947.

Lewis, Wyndham. *Time and Western Man.* New York: Harcourt, Brace, 1928.

Meyerhoff, Hans. *Time in Literature.* Berkeley and Los Angeles: U. of California Press, 1955.

Morris, Charles W. *Foundations of the Theory of Signs,* v. 1, no. 2, *International Encyclopedia of Unified Science.* Chicago: U. of Chicago Press, 1938.

————. *Signs, Language, Behavior.* New York: Prentice-Hall, 1946.

Peckham, Morse. "Metaphor: A Little Plain Speaking on a Weary Subject," *Connotation,* I (Winter 1962), 29-46.

Perry, Ralph Barton. *The Thought and Character of William James,* briefer version. New York: George Braziller, 1954.

Shattuck, Roger. *The Banquet Years: The Arts in France,* 1885-1918. New York, 1958.

Toklas, Alice B. *What Is Remembered.* New York: Holt, Rinehart & Winston, 1963.

Index

Stieglitz, Alfred
  letter from Gertrude Stein
    (May 6, 1912), 135
  Camera Work, 135
Stravinsky, Igor, 27
Stream of consciousness, 16, 134,
  207-15
Sutherland, Donald, 23, 74, 99,
  133, 210
  *Gertrude Stein: A Biography of
  Her Work,* 19, 74n., 99n.,
  181n., 209n.

Toklas, Alice B., 35n., 100, 144,
  157, 159, 175, 200, 207
Transatlantic Review, 100
transition, 176

Van Vechten, Carl, 164n., 182n.

Webster's *Third International
  Unabridged Dictionary,* 28
Weeks, Mabel, 32
Whitehead, Alfred North, 20, 27
  Principia Mathematica, 16
Wilder, Thornton, 20, 194
  "Introduction" to *Four in
  America,* 20, 194
Wilson, Edmund, 99
  Axel's Castle, 99
Woolf, Virginia, 34
  The Waves, 77

Yale Collection of American Literature, 63n., 97, 100, 100n.,
  135n., 154n.
Yale University Press, 18, 144

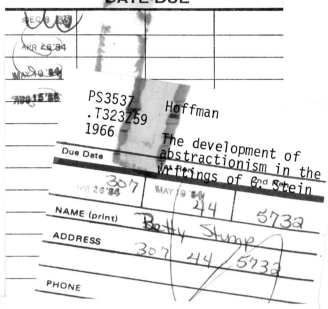